Changing the World on a Tuesday Night
Published by
Lumino Books, LLC
Denver, Colorado
www.LuminoBooks.com

Copyright © 2010, 2011 by Lumino Books
All Rights Reserved

No part of this book may be reproduced or transmitted in any form or by any means, graphic, electronic, or mechanical, including photocopying, recording, taping, or by any information storage retrieval system, without the written permission of the author.

ISBN: 978-0-9829994-0-0
Library of Congress Control Number: 2010913379

Editor: Marj Hahne
Art Direction, Cover, Interior Design and Typesetting: Amanda Oscarson
Art Direction and Interior Design: Eric Trujillo
Illustrator: Kelly Rodrigues

For more information visit: www.OnaTuesdayNight.com

Changing The World
On a Tuesday Night

Tammi DeVille

Lumino Books

How to Use This Book:

- Keep it handy. When you need a reminder that the world is full of good people doing good things, when you need inspiration or a bit of hope, read a random profile.
- Give it away to someone you know who really wants to "be the change" but doesn't know where to begin.
- Fill in the blank profile on page 130 with details about someone you know who's already *Changing the World on a Tuesday Night*. Give this book to them as a gift to honor their contribution.
- Buy a bunch for your favorite charity to use as a tool to inspire participation, and talk to them about selling the book as a fundraiser.
- Not sure where to find your "Tuesday Night"? Read this book with a highlighter in hand, and mark the lines, people, and stories that move and inspire you. It's a great way to zero in on the many ways you could contribute, find fulfillment, and have fun!

Finding your cause:

If you're not sure what your cause is or what matters most to you, the exercise on page 134 can help you discover what stirs your heart; where you feel called to contribute.

Celebrating your contributions:

If you're one of the many generous volunteers already in action, please visit us at www.OnATuesdayNight.com, where you can upload your story. And add your own profile on page 130. Part of making a difference in the world is celebrating and commemorating your work and its impact.

Maybe together we can start a revolution Maybe we can start on Tuesday.

**What are you doing this Tuesday night? How about the next?
What did you do last Tuesday?**

It's easy to get lost in the day-to-day routine, our predictable lives, easy to focus on feeding the dogs, surfing the net, paying the bills, and hitting the happy hours—but maybe, just maybe, we could, together, do something unpredictable. Maybe together, on Tuesday nights and Saturday afternoons and family vacations, we could actually change the world…change *our* world. Maybe, if we work together and each pitch in just a couple of hours a week, we can feed *all* the hungry, advocate for all the animals, support *every* kid's dream.

*This book is about ordinary people
who are making an extraordinary difference.
This book is about you being one of them.*

It's inspiring to think about being someone who changes the world. We all have things in the world we'd like to change. We can all see what's wrong. But this book isn't about what's wrong. This book is about what's right. This book is about the impulse inside all of us to make a difference in the world. This book is about the sometimes simple, always extraordinary work of people who are, literally, changing the world.

This book is about the bank vice president who says the best part of his week is the time he spends holding and comforting sick babies. And the college kid who loves helping poor families become homeowners. It's about the family who spends their vacations building villages.

In their work, they don't just change the world; they change themselves. When we give to others, we give to ourselves.

"Nobody made a greater mistake than he who did nothing because he could do only a little."
—Edmond Burke

This book is a celebration of the spirit that has people willing to change their routine, so they can change the world. That spirit is in all of us. This book is a celebration of what a single person can do. May you get inspired about the difference one person can make, the difference you can make.

There are a lot of good causes, a lot of good deeds to be done. It can be overwhelming to consider how much need there is in the world. Find your own unique way to make a difference, to share your skills and passions, to change someone's life—and yours. Find your own "Tuesday Night," your own way to change the world…and together we will.

The revolution is underway. Join us.

Find your cause.

Pick a night.

Change the world.

Table of Contents

Page	Activity	Organization
12	Answering calls	Families First of Colorado
14	Raising funds	Red Cross' Club Red
16	Cooking with kids	Common Threads
18	Organizing "no commitment" volunteers	One Brick
22	Sharing plants	Garden Partners
24	Caring for animals	New Hampshire SPCA
26	Giving career advice	Futures for Kids
28	Sending books	Darien Book Aid
32	Fighting cancer	Susan G. Komen For the Cure
34	Coordinating volunteers	Planned Parenthood
36	Creating marketing pieces	Taproot Foundation
38	Taking portraits	Project Homeless Connect
42	Sharing compassion	Concord Prison Outreach
44	Crocheting blankets	Bundles of Love
46	Being a friend	Best Buddies
48	Supporting dreams	Big Brothers Big Sisters
52	Sharing experiences	Youth Villages
54	Protecting neighborhoods	Guardian Angels
56	Coaching girls	Girls For a Change
58	Feeding children	World Hunger Relief
62	Tutoring dropouts	Operation Bootstrap
64	Supporting a community	Global Volunteers
66	Defending animals	PETA
68	Connecting kids with horses	Angel Acres
72	Serving food	Manna House
74	Visiting & playing games	Welcome House Kentucky and St. Charles Care Center

Page	Activity	Organization
76	Protecting the planet	Greenpeace
78	Preserving ecological diversity	The Nature Conservancy
82	Searching & rescuing	Minuteman Civil Defense Corps Search & Rescue
84	Building homes	Habitat for Humanity
86	Preparing for disasters	Medical Reserve Corps
88	Mentoring via webcam	Infinite Family
92	Raising puppies	Assistance Dogs of the West
94	Creating possibilities	Bridge Builders for Kids
96	Mentoring an immigrant	Pan-African Association
98	Dressing women	Dress for Success
102	Setting an example	StandUp for Kids
104	Giving music	Blind Center of Nevada
106	Translating	RESPECT International
108	Interpreting for patients	Iowa City Free Medical Clinic
112	Cuddling babies	Global Volunteers & Penn State Children's Hospital
114	Advocating for kids	CASA
116	Delivering wishes and peaceful dreams	Make-a-Wish & The Children's Hospital
118	Reading books	Beginning with Books
122	Organizing lives	Women's Bean Project
124	Teaching guitar	Guitars Not Guns
126	Baking pies	SAME Café
128	Teaching chess	Chess for Success
130	Add your story	
132	Resources	
134	Find your cause	

Forty-four percent of adults volunteer and two-thirds of these volunteers began volunteering their time when they were young. Adults who began volunteering as youth are twice as likely to volunteer as those who did not volunteer when they were younger.

Source: IndependentSector.org

> How wonderful it is that nobody need wait a single moment before starting to improve the world.
>
> — ANNE FRANK

Josie is answering calls.

FAMILIES FIRST OF COLORADO

TIME WITH THIS ORGANIZATION:
2+ years

•

HER TIME COMMITMENT:
8 hours per month (from home)

•

HER ROUTINE:
two Fridays a month, from 6:00 – 10:00 pm

LOCATION: DENVER, CO
AGE: 30
FAMILY: married, mother of two (ages 5 and 10)
OCCUPATION: child-protection case worker

A phone rings on a Friday evening in the home of thirty-year-old Josie. It's probably not a friend calling to chat or invite her to a movie. Every other Friday night, from 6:00 to 10:00, the support line for Families First of Colorado is forwarded to her home line. Who's calling? Sometimes it's a dad who needs the number of a medical clinic; other times, a teenager frustrated with his parents, who just wants to talk. Sometimes it's a mother at her wit's end with her children, who needs support in breaking the cycle of violence; other times, a lonely lady who just wants to hear a friendly voice on the other end of the phone.

Adopted as an infant, Josie reconnected with her biological parents when she was a teen. It was not a fairy-tale reunion. Those challenges inspired her to want to help others in similar situations, so Josie chose to study the field of social work. During her sophomore year in college, she was required to do a certain number of hours of community service. Researching various opportunities, she was drawn to a Families First opening, which allowed her to serve from her home. Though her school requirement has long been fulfilled, Josie continues to make this contribution to others, one she finds very rewarding and easy to keep in her life.

CHANGING THE WORLD ON A TUESDAY NIGHT

*"Some people need to get comfortable with one person," says Josie.
"They take their time to build a comfort level with you.
I'm glad I was there to answer the call."*

When Josie began volunteering with Families First, she staffed the line every Friday night. Some callers recognized that it was the same friendly voice each week, so they kept calling, no doubt taking comfort in the familiarity and the opportunity to build trust. One such "regular" was a timid girl, about sixteen years old, who shared that she was a victim of abuse by a family member. Quite reserved and very scared, she wasn't sure what to do or whom she could trust. Josie took her calls for several weeks; it took that amount of time to persuade her to tell someone, an adult in her life, that she needed help. Eventually that's exactly what she did.

In Her Own Words:

"I remember a sermon a pastor gave once. He said, 'You're always praying for other people, maybe for someone to help them, someone to intervene. Sometimes it's meant for you to help them.'"

What's the biggest thing you've learned?
"I've really realized that some people feel like they have nowhere to turn. And I've learned how easy it is to help someone else. You don't have to have a ton of time or a degree. It's just so simple that one person listening to another person can impact someone's life."

The Cause:

In Colorado, a child is abused or neglected every hour of every day. Families First offers parenting classes, a support line, and a residential treatment center focused on the prevention and treatment of child abuse. Founded in 1986, its mission is to create a community that empowers and educates parents, nurtures children, and strengthens families in a welcoming, non-judgmental way. Following the national Circle of Parents® model, Families First promotes proactive parenting and education on how to nurture, bond with, and discipline children in a healthy way. It understands that making parenting choices can be challenging, and strives to provide the community outreach, education, and support necessary to guide parents through the parenting process.

Learn more at
www.FamiliesFirstColorado.org

Photo: Eric Trujillo

When Josie isn't working or volunteering, you'll find her spending time with her kids and her husband.

Jessica is raising funds.

AMERICAN RED CROSS & CLUB RED

TIME WITH THIS ORGANIZATION:
1 ½ years

HER TIME COMMITMENT:
5 – 10 hours per month

HER ROUTINE:
1 monthly board meeting and 1 Club Red committee meeting, soliciting auction items during half of the year, attending social events with Club Red

LOCATION: ARLINGTON, VA
AGE: 30
FAMILY: married
OCCUPATION: mechanical designer, Orbital Sciences Corporation

Photo: Stephanie Miller

Deep in the Appalachian region of West Virginia, rich in natural resources but economically poor, twelve high school kids and six adult volunteers, after a week of rebuilding and repairing dilapidated homes, sat in a circle and reflected on what they'd accomplished, whom they'd helped, and the unforgettable impact the experience had made on them.

"Before the Appalachian Service Project (ASP) trips started," Jessica explains, "I, at 15 years old, had never really 'roughed it' before or seen the more difficult situations that people live in. On that mission trip, I stayed on the floor of a school gymnasium on a blow-up mattress, woke up really early, worked hard all day, and, as a result, never wanted to take for granted what I had at home. More important, I grew a compassion for those in need and wanted to give what I could while I could. The gracious people of Appalachia taught me that when you volunteer, the return is immense."

Volunteering is a lifestyle change, one Jessica made that summer when she was fifteen. She had learned about the ASP home rebuilding effort at her church—an ongoing effort whereby

CHANGING THE WORLD ON A TUESDAY NIGHT

high school students raise funds all year long and, in the summer, help rebuild the homes of needy families in the Appalachian Mountains.

Jessica finds the greatest reward in activities where she can see firsthand the impact on others. She has organized groups of colleagues to work on Habitat for Humanity projects and, for two years, volunteered as a "shopper" with Columbia Lighthouse for the Blind, helping a visually impaired man run errands. She enjoys expanding her skills and finding new and different ways to contribute to her community.

"To become a consistent volunteer, it really is a simple change. Embrace it, look at the big picture, and see that it's just a couple of hours per month of your time that can make a huge difference in your community." she suggests.

Club Red is Jessica's latest commitment. When she moved to the Washington, D.C. area, she went to VolunteerMatch.org to search for local volunteer opportunities and connect with like-minded people. There she found Club Red, a brand-new part of the American Red Cross focused on engaging young professionals in their twenties and thirties. Jessica sits on several committees, promoting Club Red, soliciting silent auction donations, and handling various other tasks for fundraising events.

IN HER OWN WORDS:
What's a way that volunteering has impacted your life?
"I've found that it's kind of addicting. You get a lot of good feelings after a project is complete; it just feels really good to give back. And if you help someone in need, they will return the favor and help someone else. It's a chain of caring that goes on and on."

*"Do all the good you can,
by all the means you can,
in all the ways you can,
in all the places you can,
at all the times you can,
to all the people you can,
as long as ever you can."*
—John Wesley

What message would you give would-be volunteers?
"You can take your volunteer experience to any level that you like. You can either make a difference to an entire community or be a hero in your neighbor's eyes, but only you can make it happen!"

THE CAUSE:
The American Red Cross is a humanitarian organization led by volunteers whose mission is to help people prevent, prepare for, and respond to emergencies. Club Red, a membership-based volunteer group for young professionals in their twenties and thirties at the Arlington County Chapter, assists in fundraising for local, national, and international causes, provides volunteer services to the community, and facilitates social networking and the educational advancement of its members.

Learn more at **www.RedCross.org**

Photo: Stephanie Miller

When Jessica isn't working or volunteering, you'll find her spending time with her family and friends or taking long bike rides.

James is cooking with kids.

LOCATION: Chicago, IL
AGE: 40
OCCUPATION: hospitality manager, Kimpton Hotels

Common Threads

TIME WITH THIS ORGANIZATION:
4 years

•

HIS TIME COMMITMENT:
3 hours per week, all day for once-a-year event

•

HIS ROUTINE:
Mondays 3:30–6:30 pm

On his one day off, James walks the half-mile from his home to the culinary kitchen at Robert Morris University. He puts on an apron and joins three other volunteers and a professional chef, as they await the arrival of sixteen eager eight to twelve-year-olds. These kids come every Monday as part of their after-school program to learn about global cultures, their customs and cuisines.

They learn about nutrition and cooking techniques, and together prepare a different ethnic menu each week, following recipes selected by the chef instructor. James helps them chop, stir, bake—and build confidence.

James' employer, Kimpton Hotels, is a huge advocate of volunteering; each hotel property is encouraged to partner with one local charity every year and support them with events and fundraising. The year James' hotel had partnered with Common Threads, a great organization that promotes nutrition, physical well-being, and cultural diversity through after-school programs, his manager approached him about helping for just a few hours, on his day off, to prepare the venue for Common Threads' big fundraising event that day. James

CHANGING THE WORLD ON A TUESDAY NIGHT

agreed, and ended up staying all day long. For the four years since, he has chaired the volunteering committee and recruited others for this annual benefit.

James was also really drawn to volunteering in the classrooms to experience firsthand the difference that was being made with the kids. When he asked the volunteer coordinator if any evening hours were available, she told him that it's an after-school program so volunteers must be there by 3:30. Because his work day typically ended at 5:30, he resigned himself to only being able to help out once a year. Three years later, however, he resolved to find a way to give hands-on help to the after-school program. He asked his boss if there was any way he could leave work a bit early one day a week. Without hesitation, his boss said, "No problem. Just make sure your work is handled." James wished he'd asked years earlier! Coincidentally, the program day has since changed to his day off.

Children who qualify for free or reduced school lunches are selected for the Common Threads program because low-income families seldom, if ever, have the luxury of being exposed to the quality and diversity of foods and ingredients used. Every week, in fourteen Chicago neighborhoods, these kids go home with the menu, a full belly, and a new perspective to digest as well.

In His Own Words:
What motivates you to volunteer?
"The clincher was knowing that what I'm giving is far more important than what I'm losing. Giving up one day for Common Threads' annual festival or three hours a week for the after-school program is really nothing on the scale of the impact it will have on the kids for years to come. You can see all the efforts trickle from the classroom to these kids' homes. I'll bet there will be some chefs that come out of this group. It's the highlight of my week."

The Cause:
Common Threads' mission is to educate children on the importance of nutrition and physical well-being and to foster an appreciation of cultural diversity through cooking. It helps bridge cultural boundaries and strengthen our global family by teaching children about their similarities and differences in the warm comfort of the kitchen. Through the simple process of preparing and sharing a nutritious meal, children who participate in these programs learn to connect with their bodies, their neighbors, and their world in bite-sized lessons.

"You are a child of the universe, no less than the trees and the stars. You have a right to be here."
— Max Ehrmann

Learn more at **www.CommonThreads.org**

When James isn't working or volunteering, you'll find him out dancing, working out at the gym, or trying new restaurants around town (volunteering with Common Threads has made him a serious foodie).

Puja is organizing "no commitment" volunteers.

LOCATION: NEW YORK, NY
AGE: 26
FAMILY: married
OCCUPATION: social worker, Spring Creek Senior Partners

No-commitment volunteering. (An oxymoron?) Socializing while volunteering. (Don't you have to give up some of your social time to make a difference?) One Brick—a volunteer nonprofit that brings together volunteers to serve other nonprofits— busts both of these myths about giving back.

ONE BRICK

TIME WITH THIS ORGANIZATION:
5 years

HER TIME COMMITMENT:
2 - 4 hours per week

HER ROUTINE:
one event per month, emails and calls to organize other event managers

Photo: Anthony Saint James

CHANGING THE WORLD ON A TUESDAY NIGHT

Puja stumbled upon One Brick five years ago when browsing VolunteerMatch.org for nonprofits in New York City. A busy college student at the time, she was seeking one-time/drop-in volunteer opportunities, as she'd come from a family of volunteers. Her doctor-brother had volunteered in a hospital when he was a teenager, and her parents have volunteered in daycare and treasury roles at their church for over thirty-five years. Puja's first volunteer gig, at age fourteen, was with Project Hospitality, in a nursing-home gift shop, preparing coffee and snacks for residents and visitors. What she remembers most is feeding ice cream to a disabled elderly woman, an impression that no doubt helped inspire Puja's decision to become a geriatric social worker.

One Brick is composed almost entirely of volunteers, with only one paid staff member, in three levels: chapter leader, event managers, and volunteers. Puja's Manhattan chapter has one leader, twenty-five to thirty event managers, and hundreds of registered volunteers, all of whom invest no more than four hours per week.

Dozens of nonprofit causes across Manhattan are supported by One Brick volunteers giving just a bit of time on an irregular basis. They sort clothing for CareerGear, do food prep and serve at Martha's Kitchen on Sunday mornings, sort baby clothes for BabyBuggy, clean up parks, and staff fundraising walks, runs and galas—all the while socializing and networking. One Brick encourages its volunteers to go out for drinks or a meal after events. Puja believes that those personal connections with other group members are what really compel volunteers to return. She calls it a "volunteering high"—that post-event feeling she gets from both making a difference and connecting with kindred minds and hearts.

*"I slept and dreamt that life was joy.
I awoke and saw that life was service.
I acted, and behold, service was joy."*
— Rabindranath Tagore

IN HER OWN WORDS:
What's a way that volunteering has impacted your life?
"My whole perspective on life has been influenced by volunteering. It's so meaningful that you can give to someone else. And it's been an incredible experience meeting so many wonderful, like-minded individuals. The connections I've made have been some of the strongest, and the people I've met have been the most fun. One Brick has given me not only job references and mentors, but also great friends!"

THE CAUSE:
Currently operating in New York, Washington, D.C., Minneapolis, Chicago, San Francisco, and Seattle, One Brick provides nonprofits with the much-needed labor to carry out their visions. Expanding the volunteer experience, One Brick proactively fosters an environment conducive to creating social and professional connections. If you're interested in starting a chapter in your city, contact their National Director, Clive, at clive@onebrick.org. A small group of committed people is all you need to get started.

Learn more at **www.OneBrick.org**

When Puja isn't working or volunteering, you'll find her hanging out with her husband or friends, watching movies, taking a yoga class, trying to learn the guitar, or riding her bike.

There are over 1.5 million nonprofit organizations in the United States. California has the most with over 91,000.

Vicki is sharing plants.

Location: Gresham, OR
Age: 47
Occupation: 911 dispatcher

Vicki wants what we all want: a happy ending. In her line of work, she hears the beginning of many a dramatic tale every day, all day. Unfortunately, a happy ending isn't as frequent as she would like. Vicki is a 911 operator. She's been at this job for over sixteen years. She used to want to know how her calls ended, but soon learned it was best not to ask. Vicki's heart yearned for a way to experience happy endings, to know that she was bringing joy and peace to the lives of other human beings.

Garden Partners

TIME WITH THIS ORGANIZATION:
1 ½ years

HER TIME COMMITMENT:
2 hours per week

HER ROUTINE:
Thursday afternoons (her day off)

Photo: Stephen Funk

CHANGING THE WORLD ON A TUESDAY NIGHT

Given her love of the outdoors and all things natural, Vicki was intrigued by a particular posting in an email of local volunteer opportunities. Garden Partners, a therapeutic gardening organization, was looking for an activities assistant on a consistent weekly basis. This wasn't what she had in mind, but she met anyway with Julie Brown, one of the program specialists. When she walked into the long-term-care facility, Cornerstone Care Option, and met the residents with whom she'd be working, she was hooked!

Most of the participating residents have some form of memory impairment, which presents unique challenges and unpredictable moments. Vicki wears shorts "as much as your UPS man does," and with her long legs and long red hair, she stands out a bit. Several times a week, one female resident asks, "How tall are you?" To Vicki's reply, she exclaims, "You've got it going on, girl!"

Vicki sets up the activities room for the week's project and then helps collect the participating residents. They've potted plants and made salsa from the red and green tomatoes they helped grow and harvest in the courtyard. Such activities stimulate their senses of taste, touch, and smell. Residents physically unable to help pot the plants can at least touch and smell the flowers or get their hands in the dirt.

Vicki enjoys getting to know the residents and learning their personality quirks. They surprise her just when she thinks she's not going to get a response. One day when Vicki was singing aloud, a woman who hadn't spoken in weeks sang along and knew every word. Another resident, sometimes hunched over in her chair so much that her forehead rests on the table, sat up, gazed at one of the flowers Vicki was showing her, and declared, "That's inspiring!" And another lady, who used to sit with her eyes closed, now can be coaxed into laughing and talking even when she shows up grumpy and resistant to participating. It's these little moments of connection that make it all worthwhile for Vicki, these little happy endings.

In Her Own Words:
What's a way that volunteering has impacted your life?

"It provides a few hours of pure joy and satisfaction. There's a little bit of an afterglow. It's just a total delight. I have yet to wake up on a Thursday morning and regret what I have to do that day. No matter how tired I may be going into it, I always come out feeling better.

I surprise myself, because if you stopped me on the street two years ago and asked me about working with this population, I would've said, 'I don't see it.' And now, not only do I do it, I love it and I look forward to it! It probably bleeds over into the rest of my life. I'm more tolerant with some folks than I would've been before.

I recently put in a flower bed and vegetable garden at my mom's house. She's seventy years old, and for the first time in years, my mom has been going into her backyard to turn on the drip hose and pick tomatoes. The other day, she took a chair and, under the shade of a tree, read a book while I weeded the garden." (Editor: Now that's a happy ending!)

The Cause:
Garden Partners provides life-giving activity to the elderly, at risk youth, and physically, mentally, and emotionally challenged individuals, enhancing holistic health and well-being. It brings therapeutic gardening to long-term care, assisted living, and Alzheimer's care facilities; community gardens; and youth treatment programs. The success of Garden Partners grows from collaborative relationships among specialists trained in Therapeutic Horticulture; volunteers, staff, and administration; family members; and community and business partners. Garden Partners enriches lives by meeting the deep human need to nurture living things.

Learn more at **www.GardenPartners.org**

When Vicki isn't working or volunteering, you'll find her rock-hounding, taking photos in nature, or gardening.

Tony is caring for animals.

LOCATION: Hampton, NH
AGE: 47
FAMILY: married
OCCUPATION: aircraft mechanic, New Hampshire National Guard

Photo: Jane Lydick Staid

NEW HAMPSHIRE SPCA (SOCIETY FOR THE PREVENTION OF CRUELTY TO ANIMALS)

TIME WITH THIS ORGANIZATION:
8 years

HIS TIME COMMITMENT:
6 hours per week

HIS ROUTINE:
Thursdays, 5:00 – 7:00 pm, Saturdays and Sundays, 8:00 – 10:00 am

Tony's an early riser, so he has no problem waking up with the sun and driving the ten miles to his local SPCA shelter every weekend morning. The dozens of cats and dogs awaiting adoption greet him with a chorus of mews and barks. He cleans cages and pens, and takes the animals for long walks

CHANGING THE WORLD ON A TUESDAY NIGHT

so they can get some exercise and fresh air. He says these are moments that bring him peace.

Tony initially volunteered just a couple of hours a week but, joyously drawn in, now participates on committees that organize the annual Pet Fest, which features adoption drives, and the Paws Walk, which raises money and awareness for the SPCA. He also makes himself available for emergencies. When Hurricane Katrina hit New Orleans, in 2005, Tony got time off from work to travel down to Louisiana to assist in the largest animal-rescue operation he has ever witnessed. Over fifteen hundred animals were brought to a makeshift shelter at the fairgrounds, though many would never be reunited with their families, who had fled to other states for higher ground. Tony was extra prepared, then, when a flood hit his town on Mother's Day a couple of years later. He and his local volunteer team sprung into action, creating emergency shelters and helping rescue lost pets and reunite them with their owners.

"Anything worth doing is worth doing right the first time."
—Unknown

Tony feels that even though animals can't express their appreciation with words, they can communicate it: "You can see it in their eyes and in their body language." He knows that his efforts, his love and attention, matter to his four-legged friends.

The Cause:

The New Hampshire Society for the Prevention of Cruelty to Animals (NHSPCA) is a community resource center that brings animals and people together through adoption, education, investigation, and sheltering services. Relying solely on community donations, the sponsorship renewals of their Adoption Angel and Education Angel members, and two-hundred-plus volunteers, the NHSPCA serves over 121 communities on the Seacoast of New Hampshire, southern Maine, and northern Massachusetts.

Learn more at **www.aspca.org**

Photo: Jane Lydick Staid

When Tony isn't working or volunteering, you'll find him skiing, working out at the gym, wood working, working in the yard, or hiking the 4000-foot peaks of New Hampshire's White Mountains.

Ryan is giving career advice.

LOCATION: CARY, NC
AGE: 28
FAMILY: married, father of two (ages 2 and 7)
OCCUPATION: video game designer, RedStorm Entertainment

Ryan loves kids. He has two of his own and was a youth minister in his former life. Now he has a career that many young boys dream of: he's a video game designer. When a co-worker mentioned that he needed help managing a busy mentoring message board hosted by Futures for Kids (F4K), Ryan jumped right in. Futures for Kids connects students with professionals working in careers they're interested in. The field of video game design is, understandably, a popular one among the kids, whose posted questions on the message board are answered by screened mentors.

FUTURES FOR KIDS

TIME WITH THIS ORGANIZATION:
1 year

HIS TIME COMMITMENT:
1½ hours per week

HIS ROUTINE:
a few minutes here and there, easily worked into his day

Photo: Dan Glasgow

CHANGING THE WORLD ON A TUESDAY NIGHT

While many of the questions Ryan fields are repetitive and predictable—about pay, hours, training, breaking into the industry—he feels it's important to give each kid a direct, specific, unique response rather than refer them to already posted answers about the topic. He answers four or five posts a day, spending five to ten minutes on each one—time he easily fits into his daily routine, given that his workday is spent at a computer screen reviewing or designing games.

Because the industry gets a bad rap, Ryan has to educate most parents at F4K career fairs about the value of video games. He's happy to promote their many purported benefits, which include improved dexterity, logical thinking, memory, self-esteem, decision making, thinking on one's feet, and creative problem solving. The field of game design is highly competitive, so he also has to reassure parents that it's a viable career option for their child; Ryan believes wholeheartedly in following one's dreams.

In His Own Words:
What message would you give would-be volunteers?
"You can get a lot more personal life fulfillment from spending fifteen minutes a day helping kids or anyone out, than from many other things in life. There are lots of opportunities out there, where you can have a small commitment and feel really good about what you've done."

The Cause:
Futures for Kids, based in North Carolina, believes that helping kids create dreams that inspire them, and giving them resources to visualize their future, keeps them engaged in completing their education. It uses technology to bridge the gap between the hopes and dreams of students and the workforce development needs of their communities. Through its online program, F4K helps students explore career opportunities that relate to their interests and passions, and identify the steps necessary to achieve success. It also connects business professionals and community members with middle and high school students statewide, regardless of location or socioeconomic background, to e-mentor the kids about their schoolwork's relevance and motivate them to stay in school and succeed.

"All we have to decide is what to do with the time that is given to us."
- J. R. R. Tolkien

Learn more at **www.f4k.org**

When Ryan isn't working or volunteering, you'll find him enjoying TV or movies at home with the family, belting out a favorite tune, or, of course, playing games!

Keben is sending books.

LOCATION: STAMFORD, CT
AGE: 16
OCCUPATION: high school student

Keben became a volunteer by accident. He loves books, so was naturally drawn when he saw a listing for a school club he assumed was a book club, called Building with Books. Renamed buildOn, it promotes volunteerism among high-schoolers and supports them in programs that raise funds for the building of schools across the globe. Students can even apply to travel to other countries to assist in the school construction. Keben, wanting only to read books, wasn't looking for a way to volunteer, but when he learned what this organization is all about, he thought that was pretty cool, too.

When buildOn's program coordinator met with the students to share the local volunteer opportunities, Darien Book Aid caught Keben's attention, of course. Their facility, chock-full of books of all sizes and types, is where he spends his Saturday mornings, fielding requests from all over the world, searching the shelves for the perfect books, packing them up, and shipping them off to Peace Corps volunteers, prisons, libraries, hospitals, and schools. With his mom's permission, Keben occasionally brings his nine-year-old brother to help out.

DARIEN BOOK AID, BRIGHTON GARDENS

TIME WITH THESE ORGANIZATIONS:
1 year, 2 years, respectively

HIS TIME COMMITMENT:
4 hours per week

HIS ROUTINE:
Fridays, 2:10 – 4:30 pm and Saturdays, 10:00 am – 12:00 pm

CHANGING THE WORLD ON A TUESDAY NIGHT

Keben has taken on the club's role of community-service officer. Every club member is required to regularly perform some type of service in their community. Keben's responsibility is to inform students about different service opportunities and manage sign-ups for group volunteering; he even places reminder calls a day ahead of certain events. After taking on this additional role, Keben wanted to lead by example by doing even more. On Fridays after school, he and a group of friends now visit a local senior center, Brighton Gardens, where they serve snacks and drinks and play games with the residents.

"Friendship is unnecessary, like philosophy, like art... It has no survival value; rather it is one of those things that give value to survival."
— C.S. Lewis

In His Own Words:

What's a way that volunteering has impacted your life?
"It makes me feel happy when I help another person. One time at Brighton Gardens, this woman came down and said her TV was broken. I asked if I could try to go fix it, and the woman at the desk said yes. So, I went upstairs, and I was able to fix it. She thanked me profusely and hugged me. It felt great helping another person."

What's the biggest thing you've learned from volunteering?
"I've learned time management. Volunteering has also taught me that I should help people, not just because I will get a reward, but because it's something you should do. I want to do it, and I feel good when doing it. Also, volunteering brings happiness to one's heart that is inexplicable."

The Cause:

Since 1949, Darien Book Aid has been sending books free of charge to economically disadvantaged areas of the world. Launched to help war-torn Europe after the Second World War, its official mission is to promote peace, friendship, and understanding through the free distribution of books. Darien Book Aid wants people in other parts of the world to know that Americans care about them regardless of the current political climate. Promoting literacy and education is the great by-product of this endeavor. Staffed entirely by volunteers, Darien Book Aid sends books to libraries, schools, community centers, and orphanages abroad, and to prisons, halfway houses, after-school programs, Native American schools, and reading programs in the United States.

Learn more at **www.DarienBookAid.org**

Photo: Lindsay Comer

When Keben isn't working or volunteering, you'll find him reading; watching NCIS, Law and Order, or the Discovery Channel; communicating with friends on Facebook; or just relaxing on his bed.

Top Five States for Volunteer Rate
1. Utah   43.5%
2. Nebraska   38.9%
3. Minnesota   38.4%
4. Alaska   38.0%
5. Iowa   37.1%

Source: VolunteeringinAmerica.gov

"The best way to find yourself is to lose yourself in the service of others."

GHANDI

Tammy is fighting cancer.

LOCATION: BATON ROUGE, LA
AGE: 40
FAMILY: married, mother of two (ages 6 and 8)
OCCUPATION: director of radiation therapy, Mary Bird Perkins Cancer Center

SUSAN G. KOMEN FOR THE CURE

TIME WITH THIS ORGANIZATION:
5 years

•

HER TIME COMMITMENT:
4 – 8 hours per week, on average

Tammy fights—at work and at her volunteer gig. She's fighting one thing: cancer. Her early work in the field of cancer treatment was hands-on, primarily with women battling breast cancer. As her career advanced her into a management role, she had fewer personal connections with the patients. Twelve years ago, however, it all got very personal. A close friend was diagnosed with breast cancer at the age of twenty-one. Tammy became one of her caregivers, intimately involved in her treatment and day-to-day battle—a battle her friend fought for seven years.

In 2003, after her painful loss, Tammy vowed to do more to proactively fight this disease. One of her fellow caregivers was the local chapter president of Susan G. Komen for the Cure. Tammy's commitment echoes that of this organization's founder, and coincidentally, Tammy's deceased friend's name was also Susan. Tammy had always attended the races, but was now ready to step up her game. She took over the role of chapter president, a very hands-on position, answering phone calls and emails, organizing fundraisers, and recruiting volunteers. During the months leading

CHANGING THE WORLD ON A TUESDAY NIGHT

up to the big annual race, her weekly commitment increases, averaging out, over the year, to between four and eight hours.

Tammy filled her volunteer ranks with some very committed folks, people with a lot at stake in this fight. One woman, who's been in treatment for six years, has helped run the race office for the past two years. At the beginning of last year's season, she had hair; by the end, she was in a wig. Her husband is the sponsor chair and handles all the chapter's online activities. "He's a huge help; he is so passionate," Tammy acknowledges. "He's in a fight for his wife, and he knows he's running out of options."

What Tammy really loves about Susan G. Komen for the Cure is that it doesn't turn anyone away, and it provides her the opportunity to make a big impact in her own community. Each chapter does fundraising locally, 75% of which stays local, with just 25% going to corporate headquarters. From that 75%, Tammy's office is able to fulfill local grant requests, many of which have been used for screening and education. They've also funded mobile units that bring health-care services to residents in impoverished neighborhoods. She finds it so rewarding to give that grant money and then see firsthand the results very soon after.

Tammy has returned to connecting with cancer patients and survivors on a personal level. She loves grants time, not only because she gets to give out money for programs, but because she gets to hear the great success stories from the previous year's grant recipients. The other stories that touch her are those of the women who call when they've found a lump and need resources, then come back to report a promising recovery after treatment. "Race day is the most amazing day," Tammy effuses. "There's the survivor march, where cancer survivors march in a huge group together. There isn't a dry eye—that's the part that's really rewarding."

"Be the change you wish to see in the world."
— Gandhi

IN HER OWN WORDS:
What's one special moment you've experienced volunteering?
"The survivor march on race day. Seeing them celebrate life and seeing how thankful they are for every moment, because they know at any minute they can have a recurrence. I get a totally different perspective on life through them."

THE CAUSE:
Nancy G. Brinker promised her dying sister, Susan G. Komen, she would do everything in her power to end breast cancer forever. In 1982, that promise became The Susan G. Komen Breast Cancer Foundation, since renamed Susan G. Komen for the Cure, now the world's largest breast cancer organization and the largest source of nonprofit funds dedicated to the fight against breast cancer, with more than $1.3 billion invested to date.

Learn more at **www.Komen.org** *or call 1-877 GO KOMEN*

When Tammy isn't working or volunteering, you'll find her scrapbooking with a group of friends—maybe even away on a weekend "crop"—or spending time with her family.

Ellie is coordinating volunteers.

PLANNED PARENTHOOD OF CENTRAL NORTH CAROLINA

TIME WITH THIS ORGANIZATION:
1 year

HER TIME COMMITMENT:
2 hours per week

HER ROUTINE:
Thursdays 4:00 – 6:00 pm

LOCATION: Durham, NC
AGE: 25
OCCUPATION: research associate, clinical trials coordinating center

As a volunteer coordinator for Planned Parenthood, Ellie does what many volunteers probably wish they could do: she multiplies herself! Well, not exactly, but she does enroll other volunteers in Planned Parenthood's mission to provide health care to people unable to receive it elsewhere. She educates inquirers about opportunities, upcoming meetings, and orientations, then matches their interests with the organization's needs. She helps the development services coordinator plan events and finds volunteers to work those events.

Ellie strongly supports women's health issues, such as having access to affordable health care and being able to choose when to have a child. When she was invited to volunteer by a Planned Parenthood staff member while attending a progressive-dinner fundraiser at her boss's home, Ellie's "yes" came easily.

Her parents have been lifelong models of volunteerism. Her dad tutored elementary school students and now volunteers with an advocacy group for residents in long-term care and for a church program that provides shelter to homeless families. Ellie's

Photo: Dan Glasgow

CHANGING THE WORLD ON A TUESDAY NIGHT

mom does a lot of volunteer work for the church as well, including serving as the chair of the Altar Guild committee.

Ellie's employer is flexible with her schedule, allowing her to leave early on her volunteer day and make up the hours on other days. Her boss and co-workers just know that she is not available on Thursdays after 3:30. Ellie encourages others to check whether their employer has any programs or incentives for volunteering, and, if not, to request a schedule that will allow flex-time.

"Go out into the world and do well, but more importantly, go out into the world and do good."
— Minor Myers, Jr.

In Her Own Words:
What's a way that volunteering has impacted your life?
"When I leave PPCNC every week, I have a nice drive home, knowing that I really contributed to the organization and feeling good about completing something I truly believe in. PPCNC staff always tell me that what I'm doing makes a difference for them."

The Cause:
Planned Parenthood of Central North Carolina (PPCNC) advocates for and provides educational and medical services to reduce unwanted pregnancy and sexually transmitted infections, especially among teens, people with limited incomes, and the uninsured. PPCNC operates health centers in Durham and Chapel Hill, serving nearly ten thousand men and women every year, seven thousand of whom are under- or uninsured. In the last eight years, PPCNC has trained, through its peer education program, more than six hundred teens to provide accurate information and referrals to their schoolmates and friends. In 2008, PPCNC volunteers logged more than two thousand hours in roles ranging from board member to mailing clerk, marketing intern to health-care assistant, and fundraising campaign chair to event volunteer.

Learn more at **www.PlannedParenthood.org**

Photo: Dan Glasgow

When Ellie isn't working or volunteering, you'll find her having dinner with friends, driving two hours to hang out on the beach with her boyfriend, doing an outdoor activity, or working out—most recently training for a half-marathon, following up a 10K race for which she raised $650 for prostate cancer research after her father was diagnosed with the disease.

Chris is creating marketing pieces.

LOCATION: SAN FRANCISCO, CA
AGE: 27
FAMILY: married
OCCUPATION: art director, VolunteerMatch.org

TAPROOT FOUNDATION

TIME WITH THIS ORGANIZATION:
1 ½ years

•

HIS TIME COMMITMENT:
5 – 10 hours per week, on average

Art is Chris' life. And it's his livelihood. After his full workday as the art director for VolunteerMatch.org, he applies his skills set to help nonprofits around the city and country powerfully communicate their message and mission.

CHANGING THE WORLD ON A TUESDAY NIGHT

With tight budgets and minimal staffing, most nonprofits can't afford to staff a graphic designer. Chris values the opportunity to fulfill that need with what comes so naturally to him: "Volunteering justifies the skills I have, in a way that money cannot. Getting paid for what you do validates your work professionally, but using that to volunteer validates it as a force of goodness, in a way that can enact change."

VolunteerMatch.org allows their employees one paid day a month to volunteer. Chris generally uses that day to meet on-site with nonprofits to discuss their graphic design needs; he then spends five to ten hours per week completing the work from home. And during the big gala fundraising seasons, he sacrifices sleep and weekends to give thirty to forty hours a week, doing all the marketing design: save-the-date announcements, invitations, programs, banner ads, and email campaigns.

When a resource like Chris exists in the local nonprofit community, word spreads fast. Chris works with many organizations that come to him through word-of-mouth and he also does volunteer work through the Taproot Foundation, an organization that connects nonprofits with teams of experienced professionals willing to donate pro bono work through structured projects which Taproot facilitates.

Volunteering for a variety of organizations has reinforced what Chris already knew: "When you work at a big company you're one piece of many. When you work for an under-resourced non-profit, which doesn't have an entire design team, your work is all the work they're going to get. I've learned that a little bit of my time can go a long way."

IN HIS OWN WORDS:
What do you think keeps people from volunteering?
"A lot of it is the fact that there's no obvious opportunity for them. If everyone was assigned something that fit their interests and skills set, I think they would do it. When push comes to shove, people have time and they would do it. The bridge between daily life and an actual opportunity that makes sense for them is just more than most people are willing to cross on their own volition. More awareness would help. I think people aren't aware of the positive impact it can make in their own life; they may see it as an obligation and more work to do. In reality, the positive benefits far outweigh the time commitments."

THE CAUSE:
The Taproot Foundation was conceived to ensure that nonprofit organizations have the infrastructure they need to thrive, given that they're the ones who tackle our world's most challenging social and environmental problems, but without the operational resources to be effective.

Every year, hundreds of nonprofits rely on the Taproot Foundation's award-winning Service Grant program to provide millions of dollars' worth of pro bono marketing, HR, IT, and strategy management consulting services.

Taproot partners with corporations, universities, and trade associations to infuse the pro bono ethic into every business profession and thereby increase the resources available to the nonprofit sector. They strive to have all business professionals, by 2020, consider pro bono work to be an integrated and esteemed part of their careers.

Learn more at **www.TaprootFoundation.org**

"Just one more thing…"
— Peter Falk as Columbo

When Chris isn't working or volunteering, you'll find him painting (see his work at www.ChrisKoehler.com), making hip-hop music, or cooking and eating anything and everything."

Joe is taking portraits.

LOCATION: SAN FRANCISCO, CA
AGE: 59 years old
FAMILY: married
OCCUPATION: artist/photographer; runs a jewelry and photography design business with his wife

PROJECT HOMELESS CONNECT

TIME WITH THIS ORGANIZATION:
4 years

•

HIS TIME COMMITMENT:
9 hours every 2 months

•

HIS ROUTINE:
one Saturday all day every two months, and several days afterwards processing & mailing portraits

"You are your brother's keeper." This belief was strongly instilled and vividly demonstrated in the poor, farm-working community of the Salinas Valley. Joe was born into a family of Mexican & Filipino farm laborers and lived in farm labor camps along with braceros. The Bracero Program was a government initiative to meet the demand for manual labor during World War II by bringing in Mexican agricultural workers. Joe remembers well how resourceful and cooperative this community was. During the winter, when there was no work, for example, bachelors would offer help or loan money to men with families.

Photo: Erica Carillo

Joe volunteered throughout his school years and, as an adult, voluntarily facilitated art and photography projects at his children's schools. But it was an invitation from his friends Phil Williams and Mara Murray that launched an opportunity that opened Joe's eyes, touched his heart, and rekindled his love of photographing faces.

Joe met Phil and Mara when their sons were in nursery school together. Phil and Mara asked if Joe, having taken portraits of the kids for the school's yearbook, could take portraits at an upcoming Project Homeless Connect event. Joe almost said no, concerned

CHANGING THE WORLD ON A TUESDAY NIGHT

he might be too busy to take on this new commitment, but agreed because he wasn't doing anything that day. The event made an impact: he's been photographing faces of the homeless for over three years now.

The Project Homeless Connect events draw 800 to 1000 volunteers and as many attendees. They're held every two months in a city building, where various business and city employees set up their services to assist the homeless community, providing everything from a mailing address to a haircut, training and job leads to HIV testing, dental care to massages.

Joe works on the Story/Portrait Project. Homeless individuals, couples, and families tell their stories, in taped interviews, of how they came to be homeless. They can choose to have their portrait taken to accompany their story. Most are able to leave an address, usually of a family member, where their portrait can be mailed. Joe's portraits express dignity and grace, a beautiful gift that the homeless predictably don't have the opportunity to receive otherwise. In his three years with the program, Joe has captured an estimated 1000 faces. You can see some of these portraits and read some of these stories on the Project Homeless Connect website.

While a student at the San Francisco Art Institute in the early '70s, Joe did a lot of documentary photography. Since earning his BFA in photography, his eye has moved to other subjects most recently landscapes and plants, as part of his art and jewelry business with his wife. Joe loves his return to portraiture, never tiring of photographing people. "There's not a face that doesn't have a story to tell," he says. In addition to personal use, his portraits have been used for publicity on bus posters and the project's website.

"If you can dream it, you can do it."
— Unknown

Joe photographs about forty people per event, and they spread the word to others. He remembers fondly a particular gentleman, with an infectious smile, whose photo had been used in marketing materials for the Project Homeless Connect events. The second time Joe saw this man, he had returned as a volunteer; and the last time Joe saw him, he was on his feet, having secured a place to live and a job at one of Joe's favorite restaurants. His dream was to become an actor, however, so he asked Joe if he could use one of the photos as a headshot. Joe processed the film and mailed him a dozen copies of the best shot, happy to play even a small part in the realization of this man's dreams and the creation of his future.

In His Own Words:
What message would you give would-be volunteers?
"I would tell them to look for whatever their strengths and talents are and find some kind of volunteerism, some venue, where they can use those. My strength is my photography, and I've found a place where I can really use it. There's always a need for volunteerism. Even in the smallest towns, there's a need you can fulfill."

The Cause:
In October 2004, 278 volunteers conducted a survey of the San Francisco homeless population, primarily located in a 60-square-block area in the Tenderloin district, where 85% of the city's social services currently exist. Project Homeless Connect now enlists over 1000 volunteers at each bimonthly event to engage homeless San Franciscans and connect them to such needed services as medical and dental care, eyeglasses, mental health, family, food, housing information, hygiene products, HIV testing, methadone, and needle exchange.

Learn more at **www.ProjectHomelessConnect.com**

When Joe is not working or volunteering you'll find him looking for creative outlets through writing, photography and graphics.

In a study of 63,000 volunteers, these are the top 3 ways they got involved:
44% took initiative and approached the organization
26% were asked by someone in the organization
14% were asked by a relative, friend or co-worker

Source: bls.gov

Bob is sharing compassion.

LOCATION: BOSTON, MA
AGE: 48
FAMILY: married, father of three (ages 14, 17, and 18)
OCCUPATION: chief advancement officer, The Jesuit Collaborative

CONCORD PRISON OUTREACH

TIME WITH THIS ORGANIZATION:
16 years

HIS TIME COMMITMENT:
7 - 8 hours per week on average

Photo: Bill Burke

When Bob was a young boy, his father would often leave the house in the evening, off to attend a town or church committee meeting or fulfill some other civic need. This was the way adults operate in the world, he thought: they support their towns and their churches; they give back. It was important role modeling, a vivid demonstration of how powerful one's actions are, much more so than words alone. Bob followed the example of his father's actions, and hopes his children will do the same someday.

Bob is the chairman and a board member of Concord Prison Outreach (CPO), but also works on the front lines. He feels that, while leadership is critical, being actively involved in CPO's activities helps him maintain perspective and contribute his best to the mission.

In the spring and fall, Bob spends one or two weekends facilitating Alternatives to Violence experiential-learning programs with other volunteers, as well as inmates who are trained to lead. He helps lead participants, usually about twenty inmates, through various exercises to become aware of their emotions and develop communication and conflict-resolution skills. Bob and his wife, Liz, also facilitate a Friday night fathers' group in the prison, on a rotating basis with another volunteer.

CHANGING THE WORLD ON A TUESDAY NIGHT

Bob is especially moved by CPO's annual distribution of holiday gift bags to the inmates. Local faith communities donate toiletries and such items as writing paper and homemade holiday cards, which are assembled into gift bags for about 1,700 inmates. It's a special opportunity for Bob and his team to greet and shake hands with each inmate as they hand out the gift bags. "Though it can be physically and emotionally draining," Bob says, "there's a very powerful and uplifting spiritual charge that comes in connecting with each person, if only for a moment. Many inmates report back that the warm smiles and kind expressions they received were the most precious gift of all." For Bob, there's no better Christmas present.

Bob is struck every single time he goes into the prison by how real and profound his experience there is. He keeps waiting for that feeling to fade but it never does—and it seems to get even stronger when the work is harder or the decision to do the work is more difficult due to time constraints or other obstacles. Were someone to ask him how he can make such a commitment, Bob would answer, "How can I not?"

He continues, "It adds life and love to my life essentially. The word I most closely associate with love is 'give.' It's receiving a gift and giving a gift in return. With inmates in prison, we're sharing our gifts and talents and pain and suffering and life lessons with each other. I walk out feeling like I've been given this tremendous gift of understanding, companionship, common experience, and humanity. We share our lives with each other."

In His Own Words:

What do you think keeps more people from volunteering regularly?

"Many people in our society suffer from 'time famine'—'just not enough hours in the day.' Lots of pressures and obstacles get in the way of giving, volunteering, and service. At the same time, many people suffer from feeling a lack of meaning or purpose in their life. There's this strange and ironic conflict between all this business of too much to do and that hunger for real meaning and purpose in life. In my experience, the way to satisfy that hunger is the opposite of what people might think. It's not doing less; it's doing more in the way of service, giving yourself to others—which may sound like more to do, but in reality, it expands the capacity of your life and fills it with what's really important."

The Cause:

The mission of Concord Prison Outreach (CPO), a volunteer, nonprofit corporation working cooperatively with the Department of Correction, is to help reduce recidivism through the development and delivery of educational and personal growth programs, principally at the Massachusetts Correctional Institution and Northeastern Correctional Center, both in Concord. CPO strives to prepare inmates for returning to society as responsible and productive citizens. To fulfill this objective, Concord Prison Outreach communicates regularly with local faith groups; recruits and supports volunteers; seeks the financial support of local faith communities, individuals and businesses; and informs the people of Concord and surrounding towns about current issues involving prisons and the criminal justice system in order to build awareness and understanding. CPO offers programs in anger management, art, book discussion, computer basics, emotional awareness, financial planning, human relationships, nutrition and fitness, poetry and creative writing, job search skills, and tutoring.

Learn more at **www.ConcordPrisonOutreach.org.**

When Bob isn't working or volunteering you'll find him playing outside!

Ruth is crocheting blankets.

Location: Eagan, MN
AGE: 48
FAMILY: married, mother of four (ages 10, 11, 15, and 18)
OCCUPATION: independent IT consultant

Ruth loves to crochet. So much so, that her family and friends requested that she not give them any more mittens, hats, or blankets. That didn't stop her, though. Ruth continued crocheting doilies, but simply hid them in a drawer. She treasured this creative outlet but was missing the joy of giving the gifts she'd poured her heart into.

Catching an *Oprah* episode about volunteering, Ruth immediately logged onto VolunteerMatch.org, flashed on the TV screen. A search for crocheting, knitting, or sewing in her zip code came up with Bundles of Love, an organization that sews blankets and baby items for babies born into poverty. Ruth was so excited to find an opportunity that could use her passion to make a difference for others, so she contacted them immediately.

Ten years later, Ruth is a regional coordinator, recruiting and managing dozens of other volunteers. She has 200 people on her area distribution list, and sixty to eighty who participate per month. Ruth is a self-professed homebody. She does much of the volunteer coordination by email or phone, right from home, where she also does most of her crocheting and sewing. She's able to spend time with her family while watching TV and crocheting or cutting patterns.

BUNDLES OF LOVE

TIME WITH THIS ORGANIZATION:
10 years

HER TIME COMMITMENT:
2 - 20 hours per week (nearly all from home)

HER ROUTINE:
weekday evenings in front of the TV or computer

CHANGING THE WORLD ON A TUESDAY NIGHT

One of Ruth's consulting clients, Blue Cross Blue Shield, really supports volunteerism. They sponsor a certain number of volunteer hours each month and even allow employees to bring their volunteer work to the office, compensating them for their donated time. One department had scheduled a work day and requested items to be cut for sewing. Working on that project, Ruth observed a transformation among the group members, historically contentious, as they focused on the difference they were making for others instead of the differences among themselves. That department now holds monthly volunteer work meetings. For Ruth, this camaraderie among her co-workers is as rewarding to witness as the outcomes of the volunteer work itself.

In addition to making standard clothing and items for babies born with nothing, Ruth creates custom items for babies who are preemies or have special needs. She created a design that met the unique needs of these tiny babies. Then she received a special request from a hospital where a baby was born with short, stiff arms. Ruth customized a design for a preemie open-front gown that was easy to get him in and out of. She had the opportunity to meet the baby and his mom at the hospital—a rare occurrence, as Ruth and her group don't normally get to see the recipients of their work. The mother was challenged to provide for her new baby along with her other children so she was, of course, very grateful; and it warmed Ruth's heart to see the direct impact of her work.

IN HER OWN WORDS:
What inspired you to volunteer?
"I felt so lucky to have everything I need. After having four kids, I really realized that, and I wanted to make a difference for those that aren't so lucky."

"Say not unto thy neighbor, go, and come again, and tomorrow I will give; when thou hast it by thee."
— Proverbs 3:2

THE CAUSE:
Bundles of Love, entirely run by volunteers, hand-makes items for infants of low-income mothers and special-needs babies, right-sized preemie clothing, and burial gowns for infants. The organization is split into work groups that meet monthly. Some volunteers bring their sewing machines and sergers and sew during the group meetings; others drop off items they finished at home. All the items are assembled into layettes at the meetings, which get distributed to various Minnesota agencies that serve families in need.

Learn more at **www.BundlesofLove.org**

Photo: Don Buettner

When Ruth isn't working or volunteering, you'll find her watching movies with her family, lobbing balls on the tennis court, curled up with a good book, or playing board games.

James is being a friend.

LOCATION: JACKSONVILLE, FL
AGE: 37
FAMILY: father of 15-year-old stepdaughter
OCCUPATION: photojournalist

BEST BUDDIES

TIME WITH THIS ORGANIZATION:
1 year

HIS TIME COMMITMENT:
4 hours per month

HIS ROUTINE:
usually every other Saturday or Sunday for two hours, and a regular phone call with his Buddy every Thursday at 8:00 pm

Photo: James Crichlow

Love and family brought James to the cause he's most passionate about. He was formerly married to a woman whose children had been diagnosed with Fragile X Syndrome, a mental impairment that ranges from learning disabilities to more severe cognitive or intellectual disabilities. Children with this syndrome often have speech impediments and tics that can scare people off, but James, after educating himself about such conditions and behaviors, learned how to relate with his step-kids and built a strong bond. He still has a strong relationship with his 15-year-old stepdaughter.

Accompanying his then-wife to the Special Olympics in Dallas, James witnessed the joy of the Olympians at their achievements and the cheers of support. This experience really lit the spark in him to help special-needs people with mental or physical disabilities.

Several years later, a coworker invited James to a social event with Best Buddies, an organization that creates one-to-one friendships, employment, and leadership development for people

CHANGING THE WORLD ON A TUESDAY NIGHT

with intellectual and developmental disabilities. When Best Buddies put a call out for Citizen Buddies, its program that matches working professionals with disabled individuals in the workforce, James attended its monthly gatherings, frequented by Buddies and volunteers. These programs have an ongoing need for volunteers; for James, it seemed like a natural thing to do. He interviewed with the coordinator and met with a few potential Buddies, including Brandon, his current Buddy. In their initial thirty minutes together, they talked a lot about photography, and James felt they really connected.

In his mid-twenties and autistic, Brandon lives with his parents and works at a local nonprofit. Acting as a friend, mentor, and confidante, James does more listening than anything else. They keep connected via e-mail, sometimes one to three times a week, and Brandon calls James every Thursday at 8:00 PM. They also get together about twice a month, on the weekend, sometimes just going to the Dollar Store—Brandon really likes that place—or eating out, at Popeye's, Hardee's, Chili's, or wherever Brandon has a coupon. They also shoot pool, go bowling, or just drive around and talk about life and goals. Brandon has big goals: he wants to learn to drive, start dating, and get a place of his own someday. James describes one particularly poignant moment: "He looked at me and said, 'I go to work and see all these guys with their girls, and people with houses and cars. When is it going to be my turn?' That really hit me: he just wants to have a normal life. I feel like I'm doing a small part in helping him get that."

In His Own Words:
Why do you volunteer?
"To be able to look myself in the mirror. When I reach the end of my life—five weeks or fifty years from now—I'll ask myself, 'Did I do enough to make this world a better place?' It's just that simple. I don't want to be a philosopher that talks about how the world is a mess but doesn't start in my little corner. I can sleep better at night, making [Brandon's] life a little better. I want to know that I left something here that will continue on. When you do your job, you want to do it to the best of your ability. Being alive, having the gift of life—I have to share that to the best of my ability, too."

What message would you give to would-be volunteers?
"The benefit, the personal enrichment, outweighs any mediocre cost of time or resources by ten-, twenty-fold. When someone realizes what you're doing for them, maybe they won't say thank-you, but even just a look of recognition, that millisecond of time, will far outweigh anything you gave up—by light years. You'll get everything out of it. You'll get the world out of it. You'll feel like you did something that mattered."

"Blessed is he who considers the poor, the Lord will deliver him in times of trouble."
— Psalm 41:1

The Cause:
Best Buddies, an international nonprofit, provides opportunities for one-to-one friendships and integrated employment to people with intellectual disabilities. Its Middle School, High School, and College Programs operate as student-run organizations and pair with the Elementary and Special Education department or a host site. Its Citizens Program connects adults in a one-to-one friendship, and e-Buddies provides a one-to-one friendship through e-mail. Its Jobs Program helps participants find lasting, integrated employment.

Learn more at www.BestBuddies.org and www.BestBuddiesFlorida.org

---

When James isn't working or volunteering, you'll find him playing with his band ("your basic Dave Matthews Band meets Foo Fighters, with a splash of Fugazi"), hanging out with the kids, or watching football.

Nancy is supporting dreams.

LOCATION: CHESTER COUNTY, PA
AGE: 45
OCCUPATION: senior communications tax research analyst

BIG BROTHERS BIG SISTERS SOUTHEASTERN PENNSYLVANIA (BBBS SEPA)

TIME WITH THIS ORGANIZATION:
4 years

HER TIME COMMITMENT:
6 hours per month

HER ROUTINE:
one Saturday per month and phone calls

Photo: Missy Sowden

Nancy had anticipated a different life at this age—that her marriage would last forever, that she would be a mom and a role model, shaping a child's future.

When her marriage ended after thirteen-and-a-half years, she felt like she'd lost herself. Sensing there was more to life, some purpose to her life, she embarked on a journey of self-discovery and self-improvement—and giving back was a big part of her process. After the tragedies of 9/11, Nancy and some co-workers started The NUF Team—"fun" spelled backwards—to bring smiles, laughter, and joy back to their workplace. They organize charity events and facilitate fun activities at the office.

Still desiring to impact a child's future, Nancy decided it was time to investigate Big Brothers Big Sisters, an organization she'd heard about for years. She says it was the best decision she's ever made.

Big Brothers Big Sisters refers to its mentors and mentees affectionately as "Bigs" and "Littles." Nancy was matched with a ten-year-old Little named Tara: "She's really bright and a lot of fun, and I adore her. She amazes me. She's become part of my family; my

CHANGING THE WORLD ON A TUESDAY NIGHT

parents think of her as a granddaughter. She asks about my going back to graduate school; we talk a lot about how that's going."

Tara lives in a single-parent home with three older brothers, so her mom registered her with BBBS to provide something just for her. Close in age, Nancy and Tara's mom have become friends.

Only recently has Tara, though very smart, indicated that she believes she can be anything she wants when she grows up. Nancy is intent on supporting Tara's new dream to be a pediatrician, finding ways to help her make it a reality.

"We make a living by what we get, but we make a life by what we give."
— Winston Churchill

The Cause:
Big Brothers Big Sisters Southeastern Pennsylvania (BBBS SEPA) is the most experienced volunteer & donor supported one-to-one youth-mentoring program in the state, matching children who need an extra friend and role model with an adult volunteer mentor. Together, they learn, socialize and share new experiences a few times each month—an investment time-proven to help keep the children in school and away from drugs, alcohol, and violence. BBBS SEPA serves thousands of children in Chester, Delaware, Montgomery, and Philadelphia Counties annually.

Learn more at **www.bbbssepa.org** *or* **www.bbbs.org**

In Her Own Words:
How has volunteering impacted your life?
"I think that it showed me how bright and tuned in kids are. Not having any myself, I'm always amazed at what little adults they are. My Little and I are growing and learning together: she's helping keep me young, and I'd like to think I'm helping her mature into a happy, responsible teen and then an adult. It's so rewarding giving back. I've learned a lot about myself. And I've met the most wonderful people along the way!"

Have you recruited others to volunteers?
"Yes, I'm always on the lookout for men who might be interested; the program always needs more men. Recently, at school, I participated in a Leadership Forum, where I discussed my Big experience. As a result of my positive experience with BBBS SEPA, two people are interested in becoming a Big. Last month, when my car service technician, Corey, found out I was a Big and heard it was one of the best things I've ever done, he signed up that night! If sharing my experience can help create new matches, then I'll keep talking about it."

Photo: Missy Sowden

When Nancy isn't working or volunteering, you'll find her spending time with family and friends, baking or cooking, attending class, doing homework, enjoying a nature walk, or taking time to "smell the roses."

59% of all volunteers who engage in mentoring work full-time.
Source: nationalservice.org

to the world **YOU MAY BE JUST ONE PERSON** But to one person, you may **BE THE WORLD**

Josephine Billings

Markus is sharing experiences.

Youth Villages

TIME WITH THIS ORGANIZATION:
1 year

HIS TIME COMMITMENT:
2 – 3 hours per week

HIS ROUTINE:
usually Saturday mornings

Photo: Youth Villages

Location: Memphis, TN
AGE: 30
FAMILY: married
OCCUPATION: sales planning manager, FedEx

Markus' family immigrated to the United States from Germany when he was just four years old. The new sights, sounds, and experiences left quite an impression, but one of the most profound had nothing to do with his new country.

Close to the interstate, Markus' new house brought not only noise but lots of wanderers into the neighborhood. One day a homeless man came to their door hungry; Markus' parents invited him in, prepared him a meal, and gave him some money. They explained to Markus that one's decisions essentially influence one's lot in life, but many people are affected by things out of their control—the opportunities they were or weren't afforded, the neighborhoods they were raised in, whether or not their parents were supportive and cared if they went to school and did their homework—that such circumstances and their consequences can have a lifelong effect, so if there's something you can do to help them out, you should. This memory and lesson remain with Markus to this day.

When Markus and his wife relocated to Memphis, they quickly observed that their new city is fairly impoverished and its problems get most of the press coverage. Having both grown up in a positive environment, their parents focused on their children's opportunities and

CHANGING THE WORLD ON A TUESDAY NIGHT

successes, taking a vested interest in their education. Many Memphis residents, children especially, don't get those same opportunities, through no fault of their own. So serving as a role model and providing positive reinforcement is something Markus and his wife are very passionate about.

A recent job change finally gave Markus the time and space to commit to volunteer for Youth Villages, a private nonprofit organization dedicated to helping emotionally and behaviorally troubled children live successfully. He mentors a 13-year-old boy with Asperger's Syndrome, who has difficulty managing his emotions, particularly anger. He goes home every third weekend to see his parents, who live 300 miles away, so his only self-directed outings are those with Markus every week or two—a Memphis Tigers basketball game, go-karting, a restaurant, whatever he wants to do. Markus' job is to be a role model, an ear, a non-authoritarian chaperone, a friend. When they talk about issues that arise and how he copes with his anger, Markus relates his own life challenges and resolutions.

During the mentor application process, the staff had warned Markus to not be surprised if it takes several visits to gain trust and create a connection with the mentee. During the matching meeting, after some icebreakers, the liaison and counselor left Markus alone with his potential mentee. They walked together and talked about their families. Markus was nervous, sure that the boy was sizing him up, wondering if this is someone who really has an interest in him. Just as they were finishing their visit, the boy looked up at him and asked, "Can I see you again tomorrow?"

"The challenge is what drives me crazy, but it is also what drives me."
— Prescott Hoffman

In His Own Words:

What's a way that volunteering has impacted your life?
"It never ceases to amaze me the sheer joy on his face when the staff brings him from his cabin to the admin building, where I pick him up. He's smiling from ear to ear, excited for anything that we do, even things that seem mundane and ordinary to me. Last night I said, 'What do you want to do?' He wanted Chinese food, and 'After that,' he said, 'can we go walk around Wal-Mart?' It doesn't matter what we do. Here I was, racking my brain trying to think of things to do—the zoo, museum, sports games—but it doesn't matter how great the event is, all that seems to matter to him is spending time with someone who cares and is taking time out of their day. It's a humbling experience to see the difference a little time makes. When was the last time I had such joy about just going to Wal-Mart?"

What do you think keeps people from volunteering?
"If they're like me, it's probably an overestimation of the time commitment. It's really not as much time as you think and, more importantly, you'll never miss what you're giving up. I would say, 'Do it.' You can't possibly imagine the impact you'll have for how little you put into it."

The Cause:

Youth Villages, a private nonprofit organization, helps more than twelve thousand emotionally and behaviorally troubled children and their families, in ten states and the District of Columbia, each year. An early champion of research-based treatment approaches, Youth Villages aims to create the least restrictive setting, especially through intensive in-home counseling services. This family-centered approach has produced consistently high long-term success rates unheard of in the industry, and has earned Youth Villages national prominence as one of the country's leading children's behavioral health organizations. Its other services include therapeutic foster care, mentoring, adoption, and residential treatment.

Learn more at **www.YouthVillages.org**

When Markus isn't working or volunteering, you'll find him traveling the globe with his wife, Stacie.

John is protecting neighborhoods.

LOCATION: PEA COUNTY, MD
AGE: 39
FAMILY: married, father of three (all in their 20s)
OCCUPATION: city bus driver

Some people make a difference merely by their presence, by just showing up with commitment and heart. John has been showing up for almost twenty-five years.

At fourteen, on the streets of his New York neighborhood, John first encountered the group of men that would change his life forever. Seeing them from afar, dressed alike in their red berets, walking with intention around the block, he initially thought they were part of a gang. When he went over to talk to them, to see what they were up to, they said they were looking for a missing child. He concluded that they were kind of like a gang, except their goal was to protect those who couldn't protect themselves.

Shortly thereafter, John enrolled himself in the martial-arts training program of the Guardian Angels. He continued training and patrolled his hometown until the age of nineteen—at which time, it became apparent that a Guardian Angels chapter was sorely needed in the nation's capital. Relocating for the sole purpose of continuing the organization's work there, John found jobs in building management and maintenance and now drives a city bus. No matter how he makes his living, John has clearly given not just his evenings, but really his life, to the Guardian Angels.

Photo: Stephanie Miller

Since 1989, the Washington, DC chapter has made its presence known in various neighborhoods throughout the city. The Guardian Angels show up where crime shows up, acting as a visual deterrent. They respond to requests from citizens in areas where crime sprees or tragic incidents—a string of robberies, a rape, a murder, increased drug dealing—have occurred. They assist in searches for missing persons,

GUARDIAN ANGELS

TIME WITH THIS ORGANIZATION:
over 24 years

•

HIS TIME COMMITMENT:
20 hours per week on average

CHANGING THE WORLD ON A TUESDAY NIGHT

attend or host vigils, pass out flyers to educate citizens, and conduct Citizens on Patrol training. They participate in community events like the MLK Parade, Unifest, Black Family Reunion Day, and Adams Morgan Day.

City councilmen acknowledge the Guardian Angels' work and welcome their presence. In fact, John's chapter achieved two firsts in the organization's history. Says the Guardian Angels website, "Because of Mr. Ayala's work in Washington, his was the first chapter to be issued a police radio from the police chief, and is the first chapter to go through the police academy."

Among the chapter's twenty-four members, the youngest is sixteen and the average age is thirty. "A lot of kids in the community want to know what we're about," John says. "We're not in the papers and not known as much with this generation. A lot of young people nowadays are hooked on gangs, cliques, crews as a second family, as protection, and we try to change their mindset. We teach them that you can have all those things but, in the Guardian Angels, we put it towards being positive and not predatory."

This cause is clearly not for everyone; though nine out of ten times, "nothing happens" on patrol, it's not without danger. During his time in DC, John has been stabbed once and incurred a second knife wound at the hands of a drug dealer. These incidents don't rattle him; he believes strongly in his mission to deter crime and keep the streets safe.

In His Own Words:
What's the biggest thing you've learned from volunteering?
"Being involved in the community is very important; if you don't get involved and you lock your doors and pull your shades, you're going to have more crime in your community. Criminals can't come into your community and control it if they know your community is too active."

"Dare to care."
— Unknown

What message would you give would-be volunteers?
"If you're thinking about it, follow your heart. See what types of organizations you enjoy."

The Cause:
With 136 safety-patrol chapters throughout the world, the Guardian Angels remains a volunteer-based organization that includes inner-city youth, empowering them to be part of the solution in cleaning up their communities. On call 24/7, Guardian Angels are trained in CPR/First Aid, self-defense, and what to do if they see a crime in progress; they are trained to make a citizen's arrest if needed. They attend large community gatherings to deter criminal disruptions and provide community services, such as distributing food to the hungry and homeless, and speaking to elementary, junior high, and high school students about the dangers of gangs, drugs, peer pressure, and the importance of staying in school.

Learn more at **www.GuardianAngels.org**

Photo: Stephanie Miller

When John isn't working or volunteering, you'll find him spending time with friends or family at the movies, a nightclub, a restaurant, or a play.

Sarah is coaching girls.

LOCATION: PHOENIX, AZ
AGE: 31
FAMILY: mom to one dog, a Weimaraner named Lilly
OCCUPATION: manager of account development, American Express

FLORENCE CRITTENTON OF ARIZONA, GIRLS FOR A CHANGE

TIME WITH THESE ORGANIZATIONS:
2 years

HER TIME COMMITMENT:
8 - 10 hours per month

HER ROUTINE:
meets with her mentee two times a month, holds an after-school program for Girls for a Change two times a month

Photo: Pamela Nicole Bernasconi

If Sarah's childhood had been less challenging she says, she might not have grown into someone always looking for ways to make a difference. Her mother's mental illness and her family's numerous relocations had taken their toll on thirteen-year-old Sarah. When she began acting out, a school counselor, Keith Donaldson, took a very active role in her life, working with her one-on-one and coaching her in group settings. Realizing that "somebody does care about me," she changed her attitudes and her actions.

Now as an adult, Sarah wants to give that same kind of support and encouragement to young people. Her two volunteer gigs allow her to pay it forward in different, but equally meaningful, ways. With Florence Crittenton of Arizona, Sarah is that solid support system for a young girl experiencing a challenging childhood. And, with Girls For A Change, she proactively educates and directs young girls who are at-risk.

Sarah was a bit hesitant to take on the role with Girls For A Change, because some of

CHANGING THE WORLD ON A TUESDAY NIGHT

its activities occasionally overlap with work time. She was able to make schedule arrangements easily, however, because her employer, American Express, has a strong commitment to volunteerism and a good work—life balance—so much so that a volunteer web portal can be accessed through the company intranet.

Twice a month after school, Sarah and another volunteer facilitate a team of twenty to forty, twelve- and thirteen-year-old girls, primarily high-risk. They discuss current social issues, some of which are brought up by the girls. They then lead the girls through the process of creating projects that can improve the day's issue, thereby teaching these girls that they can positively impact the circumstances affecting them and their communities.

With Florence Crittenton, Sarah mentors a fifteen-year-old girl who, at age five, had been adopted from China. Also struggling with mental illness, she began acting out in her early teens; she has run away from home and has been incarcerated. Sarah's own childhood experience gives her a great deal of empathy for her mentee. They talk a couple of times a week by phone, and meet in person twice a month, spending time together at the library, going out to dinner, or just chatting.

In Her Own Words:

How has volunteering impacted your life?

"It gives me a heightened sense of empathy for people in need. When I observe children who act out, I know that if you get in there, get familiar with them, and allow them to get comfortable enough with you, you'll learn that there are things out of their control impacting them. If you see a homeless guy on the street, a common first reaction is to think he must be lazy and doesn't want to work, but when you get to know some of the stories, you may begin to understand the circumstances."

"Life isn't about waiting for the storm to pass; it's about learning how to dance in the rain."
— Unknown

What is a special moment you've experienced volunteering?

"Every time I get off the phone with my mentee, she says, 'I love you. Talk to you later.' I just love that, that I'm someone she can count on and can relate to like that. I can see her attitudes and perceptions changing."

The Causes:

Florence Crittenton of Arizona has served Arizona's youth and their families for more than a century. Its comprehensive continuum of care helps at-risk girls from twelve to twenty-one overcome issues of abuse, neglect, teen pregnancy, teen parenting, and behavioral and/or mental health problems.

Learn more at **www.FloCrit.org**

Girls For A Change (GFC) is a national organization that empowers girls to create social change by designing, leading, funding, and implementing projects that tackle the issues they face in their own neighborhoods. It provides the tools, resources, partnerships, and support girls need to gain the voice, ability, and problem-solving capacity to realize their full potential. GFC welcomes and serves all girls, focusing its efforts on those who live in low-income communities.

Learn more at **www.GirlsForAChange.org**

When Sarah isn't working or volunteering, you'll find her hanging out with her friends, enjoying good food and conversation, hiking with her dog, or playing in a softball or bowling league.

Sherry is feeding children.

LOCATION: LOUISVILLE, KY
AGE: 33
FAMILY: married
OCCUPATION: administrative assistant, Yum! Brands

Sherry works for the corporation that brings America popular quick-serve concepts like Taco Bell, Pizza Hut, and KFC. One company benefit she enjoys is the built-in opportunity to give back, via Yum! Brands World Hunger Relief program. Sherry could jump in and participate in existing initiatives or find a new way for her and her coworkers to contribute to this global effort.

WORLD HUNGER RELIEF

TIME WITH THIS ORGANIZATION:
3 years

HER TIME COMMITMENT:
5 hours per month

HER ROUTINE:
once a month

Photo: Sarah Hester

CHANGING THE WORLD ON A TUESDAY NIGHT

With a brother-in-law who works as a principal in the Louisville school district, Sherry thought it would be really great to involve the local school children in the World Hunger Relief fundraising efforts. His school welcomed the invitation to participate, as it was already actively seeking ways to be more involved in the community.

With school administrators, Sherry and her team created a program whereby the students collected money to feed kids a world away, in Africa. Each student was given a cup that came from Kenya, indicating the amount of food that one child gets in a whole day, to take home, fill with change from their family, neighbors, and friends—anyone who wanted to donate—then empty into a KFC bucket in their classroom. Sherry and her team created a contest to encourage friendly competition: the classroom that collected the most money by the end of the week won a pizza party. The program's goal was to raise $500—the amount collected by one fifth-grade class alone. To everyone's amazement and delight, the school raised a total of $2200!

Sherry was especially inspired by a boy whom she'd overheard say, "I'm going to take my piggy bank and bring in my whole $50. I want to be able to feed a child and say that I did it." She reflects, "They want to bring all that they have to say they made a difference. This child was willing to give $50, and sometimes we adults struggle with giving a dollar. They are so humble, innocent, and sweet."

Moved by the children's excitement and commitment, and the overwhelming success of this pilot program, Sherry and her team are now creating strategies for expanding this effort to other schools in the district, and beyond.

*"For I know the plans I have for you,"
declares the Lord,
"Plans to prosper you and not to harm you,
plans to give you hope and a future."*
—Jeremiah 29:11 NIV

Another outcome is that the kids in Louisville wanted to connect more with the kids in Africa, so they sent photographs and drawings. To maintain that connection year-round, the school administrators are pursuing the possibility of adopting an African school.

When Sherry visits her brother-in-law at the school, she's stopped by kids in the hallway who say, "I remember you. I remember we helped those children, and I still have my cup."

In Her Own Words:
How has volunteering impacted your life?
"It humbles me; it puts me at a different level of thinking; it makes me appreciate what I have. And, being able to touch someone else's life, seeing reality and the way things are for other people, I realize my problems are not big."

The Cause:
Yum! Brands annual World Hunger Relief campaign is the world's largest private-sector hunger-relief effort to raise awareness, volunteerism, and funds to benefit the United Nation's World Food Programme and other hunger-relief agencies. More than 36,000 company and franchised restaurants—KFC, Pizza Hut, Taco Bell, Long John Silver's, and A&W—in more than 110 countries, participate in the World Hunger Relief.

Learn more at **www.FromHungerToHope.com**

When Sherry isn't working or volunteering, you'll find her reading inspirational books or spending quality time with her family.

The biggest difference between those who volunteer regularly and those that do not is that those who volunteer watch about an hour less of television a day.
Source: volunteeringinamerica.gov

> You must be the change you wish to see in this world.
>
> — Mahatma Gandhi

Nancy is tutoring dropouts.

LOCATION: MARBLEHEAD, MA
AGE: 58
FAMILY: married, mother of a 29-year-old daughter
OCCUPATION: product manager, General Electric

OPERATION BOOTSTRAP

TIME WITH THIS ORGANIZATION:
15 years

•

HER TIME COMMITMENT:
2 hours per week

•

HER ROUTINE:
Mondays 5:00 – 7:00 pm

Photo: Bill Burke

Nancy believes that if your life and successes have come fairly easy, you need to give back to those who haven't had it so easy. Her parents had paid for her good education, so she clicked right away with Operation Bootstrap's mission to provide educational services to educationally and economically disadvantaged adults.

It's been fifteen years since Nancy first read about Operation Bootstrap in her company's monthly email about different causes and volunteer opportunities. At the time, she'd been actively looking for an organization to get involved with, having more time to devote to service outside the home once her daughter was in high school. She estimates she's tutored seventy-five GED students so far.

Volunteers receive no formal training; they just jump right in. It usually takes about two years for the students to pass all five required tests: a math test, three

CHANGING THE WORLD ON A TUESDAY NIGHT

basic reading comprehension tests, and a grammar test, which includes writing an essay.

Nancy feels this work has really expanded her perspective, exposing her to a part of society that had rarely entered her comfortable life. The stories of her underprivileged students are sometimes tough to hear—the reasons they dropped out of school, from probation to teen motherhood. Watching them come back from such difficult circumstances inspires Nancy and reminds her that her life is not so hard, that she, indeed, has been very fortunate.

Nancy was particularly moved by a student who received her GED in her fifties, having worked diligently to pass all her tests. She'd discontinued her education when she became a mother at a very young age. Nancy was happy to attend the graduation ceremony, hosted by Operation Bootcamp, and the woman was so pleased with her accomplishment that she introduced Nancy, her tutor, to every one of her guests. Nancy says, "Many younger people do this because they have to, to get a job. But in these cases where someone is doing this as a personal goal, a personal accomplishment, I admire them just as much."

"We must be prepared to make the same heroic sacrifices for the cause for peace that we make ungrudgingly for the cause of war."
—Albert Einstein

In Her Own Words:
What message would you give would-be volunteers?
"I don't think you can really appreciate what it's all about until you do it. You give to those who depend on you, like your family, but that's very different. This is something you don't have to do, but you do it because you want to. It's very satisfying. You do it out of yourself. You didn't write a check; you actually did something for someone when you didn't have to."

The Cause:
Operation Bootstrap offers ongoing classes in three program areas: Adult Basic Education, Adult Secondary Education, and English for Speakers of Other Languages. In addition to core instructional offerings, it provides a range of supplemental educational services, such as employment/career readiness, computer-assisted instruction, family literacy, citizenship, student leadership, and community participation. Operation Bootstrap serves the most educationally and economically disadvantaged adults in a community: youth (sixteen or older) who have dropped out of school, adults who don't have a high school diploma, and immigrants who don't speak English. The center serves four hundred to six hundred community residents annually, seventy-seven percent of whom identify as ethnic/cultural minorities, including Asian, Hispanic, and African-American.

Learn more at **www.OperationBootstrapLynn.org**

When Nancy isn't volunteering or working, you'll find her cooking for her family and friends, gardening in the flower beds in the backyard, or reading novels.

The Ross Family is supporting a community.

LOCATION: TWIN CITIES, MN
OCCUPATION: Margy (mom): international IT consultant, Scott (dad): general counsel for a tech company, Katie: high school student

GLOBAL VOLUNTEERS

TIME WITH THIS ORGANIZATION:
6 years

THEIR TIME COMMITMENT:
2 weeks per year

THEIR ROUTINE:
annual family vacation

The Ross family is a busy one. Margy—mom, wife, and international IT consultant—spends three weeks a month traveling, domestically and abroad, for her job. Scott—dad, husband, and general counsel for a tech company—endures a rigorous training schedule for Ironman triathlons. Katie, daughter, and student, is busy with schoolwork, athletics, and social activities. Quality family time is hard to come by, so vacations together are very important.

"We live in the suburbs; it's a nice life, but there's not a whole lot of 'heavy lifting' in our lives," says Margy. So when Scott didn't have much vacation time back in 2004, she planned a mother-daughter trip that involved manual labor along with a cultural experience. Googling "international volunteering" yielded Global Volunteers, which organizes group "volunteer vacations" in nineteen countries.

Photo: Dan Buettner

They ended up working on a building project for a local high school in Costa Rica, clearing a plot of ground, mixing cement by hand, and digging the foundation. They really loved being part of the tiny local community and part of a team with like-minded people from different countries and walks of life.

CHANGING THE WORLD ON A TUESDAY NIGHT

Six months later, for their Christmas trip, at Katie's insistence, they went back, taking Scott this time. Since then, the Rosses have made seven trips to this community on their annual summer vacation—two weeks that are nonnegotiable despite their work, travel, and school schedules. Margy says, "It's almost like summer camp for the family."

For Scott, this kind of volunteer work is unique not only in its opportunity to give back but also in the personal satisfaction: "You can really see the fruits of your labor, doing a tour in the community, and you can see all the projects—school dining room, irrigation ditch, community center," says Scott. "It's work that you feel good about emotionally, mentally, and physically. It has a tangibility. It's very rewarding. And one of the attractions is maintaining contact with a particular community; it's great to see the kids grow up, […] the community transform into a better place."

Katie especially values Global Volunteers' operating principle called 'match labor': "It has to be one-to-one volunteers to community members, working directly with volunteers on projects. The community determines what and how it will be done. Even if you're a civil engineer, you take direction from the community. You're in close proximity with someone who has something at stake."

An especially memorable experience was their bedside visits with a community leader, bedridden and fighting terminal stomach cancer, who was their "go-to guy" as the local organizer of the community volunteers. "When we went back the next summer," Margy reports, "Roberto was about a third the size he was when we'd seen him in December. He was very withered and confined to his bed, but he wanted us to visit. Katie and I visited every day for fifteen minutes. He was very sick, but he always rallied to see us. On the last night of our trip, we stopped at Roberto's house. It was our last opportunity to see him. He told us that some of his favorite memories were working with Global Volunteers and how appreciative he was and thankful that he was leaving his community in such a better place because of the work he could do with Global Volunteers."

In Their Own Words:

What do you think keeps people from volunteering?
Katie: "A lot of volunteer work involves emotional investment, and it's scary for people to put so much of their heart into something like this. It's hard to leave after two weeks; it's hard to say goodbye. Every year, I cry when I leave, but I'm always really proud of what I did and glad I went."

What would you say to others who might be considering a volunteer vacation?
Scott: "It's actually fun and relaxing—and less expensive than many other [vacation] options. We stay in adequate accommodations; there are no 300-count sheets, but it's a great way to model some great behaviors for your kids. I never expected this to have the impact it's had on Katie. She's now taking two language classes in high school and exploring international development as a potential major in college."

The Cause:

In its 27th year, Global Volunteers is the pioneer in short-term, community-driven service opportunities, or "volunteer vacations." Based in St. Paul, Minnesota, Global Volunteers wages peace and promotes justice through the mutual understanding arising from shared work projects in nineteen countries worldwide. Work projects include teaching conversational English, caring for at-risk children, construction and light labor, and assisting with health care.

Learn more at **www.GlobalVolunteers.org**
or call (800) 487-1074

Melissa is defending animals.

PEOPLE FOR THE ETHICAL TREATMENT OF ANIMALS (PETA)

TIME WITH THIS ORGANIZATION:
5 years

HER TIME COMMITMENT:
20 hours a week, 85% online

LOCATION: LOS ANGELES, CA
AGE: 31
OCCUPATION: emergency room nurse

Melissa vividly remembers the day, eleven years ago, she saw videos depicting the horrible conditions endured by animals raised for food. She became a vegetarian instantly. Educating herself about animal-protection causes and where her food comes from, she took the final leap to become a vegan four years later.

Melissa knew she wanted to really be a part of this cause, to educate others about it, after meeting some folks from PETA at an animal-rights conference. Wanting to do more than give money, she put herself on PETA's mailing list and began receiving regular communications with information about various issues and invitations to participate hands-on.

With greater knowledge and an active like-minded community, Melissa could do more than just think about the cause she believes in she could do something about it. Before, she didn't really know how to get involved, though she knew she felt the same way as the PETA demonstrators: "You can honk your horn when you see them on the street corner—that's easy to do—and then it's easy to get distracted by other things in your life. You forget, and eat a hamburger for lunch."

CHANGING THE WORLD ON A TUESDAY NIGHT

One particular email invitation, received a few months after joining PETA's mailing list, was Melissa's next turning point. Thrilled that people were becoming educated about these newly exposed issues, she attended a demonstration at a fast-food restaurant that allegedly supported sources mistreating animals. Since then, she has protested fur wearing just a billboard sign, been wrapped in cellophane on a human-sized foam "meat" tray displayed on the sidewalk in summer heat, painted her body like a tiger and sat in a cage to protest the circus, worked with celebrities, and spoken at city council meetings. These are things she does only for the animals. She's traveled all over the country to educate people about vegetarianism's impact on animals, the environment, and their health. If she can change just one person's opinion, it's worth it. Having received emails from folks saying she's changed their life, she knows she's achieved her goals.

As an emergency room nurse, Melissa saves human lives for a living, and now she spends the majority of her off-hours saving animal lives as well. In addition to her highly visible public activities, she spends about twenty hours a week online, bringing her activism to social networking sites. She answers emailed questions and shares information with people who are interested in animal rights, gratified to provide others what she wishes she knew years ago.

"Growing up, I didn't know about PETA or animal rights, I didn't know what I was eating, and that makes me want to be out there educating people. No one shared this information with me; and I think, if I had known then what I know now, I would've been vegan long ago." Follow Melissa online at www.myspace.com/vegan_mel, www.facebook.com/melissasehgal, and www.twitter.com/vegan_mel.

"Perhaps the Animal Spirit is so great that one day it may inspire compassion in the human heart"

— Nan Sea Love

In Her Own Words:
What's a way that volunteering has impacted your life?

"I feel like volunteering completes me. I grew up being shy and not as confident as I am now. It brought up a vocal strength I didn't know I had. I've done interviews and talked to media. I talk to all kinds of people all the time with this work. It has strengthened me and allowed me to realize what a passionate person I am."

"Whatever I'm going through in my life is nothing compared with what the animals are going through. If a week goes by and I haven't done anything, I have to do something."

The Cause:
People for the Ethical Treatment of Animals, based in Norfolk, Virginia, with affiliates in the United Kingdom, Germany, the Netherlands, India, and the Asia-Pacific Region, has been dedicated to establishing and defending the rights of all animals since 1980. Operating by the simple principle that animals are not ours to eat, wear, experiment on, or use for entertainment, PETA educates policymakers and the public about animal abuse and promotes kind treatment of animals.

Learn more at **www.peta.org**

When Melissa isn't working or volunteering, you'll find her studying paranormal phenomena or hanging out with her animal companions.

Lori-Lynn is connecting kids with horses.

ANGEL ACRES

TIME WITH THIS ORGANIZATION:
1 year

HER TIME COMMITMENT:
3 ½ hours per week

HER ROUTINE:
Saturdays,
9:00 am - 12:30 pm,
October through May

Photo: Pamela Nicole Bernasconi

LOCATION: GOODYEAR, AZ

AGE: 49

FAMILY: married, mom of two cats

OCCUPATION: fuel supply analyst for a public utility company

Every Saturday, from October to early May, Lori-Lynn drives the seventy miles to the stables at Angel Acres to spend her morning with JR, Boss, Cochise, Pete, Charlie, and Rip, six old horses who love what Lori-Lynn loves: working with kids.

Angel Acres serves at-risk and special-needs children with activities, on and off the horse, that enhance balance, muscle strength, coordination, focus, listening skills, and self-esteem.

The children begin their day grooming their horse, which bonds them to another living being. They then get on for the ride with a riding buddy, a beanie baby they insert in the loop on their therapeutic riding pad. For a warm-up, Lori-Lynn puts the children through Simon Says movements while riding facing front, sideways, and backwards, which exercises several muscle groups. She then guides them through educational games using numbers, colors, letters, shapes and memory.

When not on the horse, the children participate in art projects at the art table or play in the petting zoo with

CHANGING THE WORLD ON A TUESDAY NIGHT

the four resident goats, Jake, Rosi, Lilly, and Sweet Pea. During lunchtime, the children and volunteers eat together and discuss their favorite parts of the morning.

Lori-Lynn has always loved working with kids. She spent three years tutoring second- and third-graders in inner city schools for an hour and a half each week—an opportunity she'd learned about in a newspaper article. A company email listing volunteer opportunities is how she learned about Angel Acres, and she was immediately drawn to the idea of spending some time with horses and kids. A particularly poignant moment with an older boy in the program illustrates the magic of that alliance: "It was rewarding to speak to him each week and see him think about the horses as living beings to be cared for. I especially enjoyed having him 'sweet talk' his horse while he groomed it before the rides. He said he'd never heard of 'sweet talking' and wanted to know what that meant. When I told him that horses love to hear secrets that no one else knows and like to be told they're handsome and strong, his eyes got big. He was surprised that the horse enjoyed being groomed and talked to, so I showed him how to know if the horse is happy and listening to him. I think he had a wonderful moment thinking about having a horse as a confidant and what things he could share with it! I never did hear his secrets each week, but I'm sure the horse may have had good old-fashioned, horse-sense advice for him!"

In Her Own Words:

What's a way that volunteering has impacted your life?
"I get so much enjoyment out of knowing that I'm helping someone else. It gets me out of being self-centered to being more concerned about how I can help others. I always feel replenished after I do those things."

Do you have friends and/or family who volunteer with you?
"I would like to get my department at work to all volunteer together at Angel Acres. I did recruit my husband into tutoring, he just started this fall. He was not an easy recruit, but he's now really focused on helping his student overcome her challenges. He's very serious about figuring out how to become a better tutor so she can become a better reader."

What is an impactful or special moment you've experienced while volunteering?
"The first time I started doing tutoring I was working with a 3rd grader, a little Hispanic boy who I was tutoring in ESL (English as a Second Language). When we were done with our session, he left, walked away and then he stopped, turned around and walked all the way back and said to me 'Thank you Miss Lori.' He was just so genuine in that he appreciated what I was doing, it was from his heart and I could feel that."

The Cause:
Angel Acres, Inc. provides fun and exercise therapy on horses to children who are disadvantaged or disabled. In its six years of operation, this all-volunteer organization has given 1944 rides.

Learn more at **www.AngelAcres.org**

Photo: Pamela Nicole Bernasconi

When Lori-Lynn isn't working or volunteering, you'll find her reading, hiking, attending museums and festivals, or engrossed in arts and crafts.

With a volunteer rate of 43.9%, Utah is the top ranking state in the nation for volunteering. Utah also ranks #1 in volunteer hours, with the average volunteer serving 81.3 hours per year.

Source: volunteeringinamerica.gov

Manna House

TIME WITH THIS ORGANIZATION:
1 year

HER TIME COMMITMENT:
3 hours a week

HER ROUTINE:
Mondays 4:30 - 7:30 pm

Angelina is serving food.

Location: Madison, AL
AGE: 49
FAMILY: married, mother of three (ages 10, 13, and 16)
OCCUPATION: associate broker, Keller Williams

Photo: Nicole Allen

Angelina's family celebrates with food, shows their love with food, and always had enough food for the five of them. She remembers, "My mother always had a pot of food on the stove. She'd feed neighbors and anyone who came by."

So, when Angelina and her husband joined The Rock Family Worship Center in Madison, Alabama, she naturally got involved in its Manna House Food Distribution Center.

Several different programs operate out of Manna House. Initially, Angelina volunteered with the Backpack Program, since renamed the Phoenix Program, packing bags to put in the backpacks of local schoolchildren identified by teachers as not having enough to eat at home. Packed on Wednesdays, the bags include Friday dinner, weekend breakfasts and lunches, and snacks like fruits, beanie weenies, cheese, crackers, and sunflower seeds. Another group of volunteers delivers the bags, discreetly, to the kids at school. Angelina now helps with general meal service, providing prepared foods that people in need can take home, plus boxed goods, hamburger, chicken, chicken nuggets, and other items that can be prepared at home. One volunteer makes stews and soups that are distributed in Tupperware.

CHANGING THE WORLD ON A TUESDAY NIGHT

Angelina was immediately moved by her experiences at Manna House, and continues to be touched by the people she meets there—men, families, single women with babies. It's what keeps her coming back, week after week: "You hear about people living in tent cities, but until you see it, you might not understand. I feel like I'm needed here." Very supportive of Angelina's volunteer work, her husband stays home with the kids while she's at Manna House, and her oldest daughter has joined her a few times.

This kind of volunteer work keeps Angelina mindful to not take things for granted. She marvels, "People are so grateful for just a bologna sandwich. They say things like 'God bless you' and 'You don't know how much this means.'" One particular moment that made her really proud was when a woman came in on a very cold day with her two little girls and her six-month-old baby, who had no shoes or hat. Angelina thought to herself, "That baby needs some shoes." Another volunteer had already noticed and went and found some shoes in the adjacent clothing ministry. Angelina explains, "She didn't say a word; she just went over and played with the baby and put them on, without making a big deal or making them feel 'less than.' A lot of what this ministry does is it gives them their dignity back. We let them select their own food; we respond with 'Yes, ma'am' and 'Yes, sir.' I think it adds to their well-being."

In Her Own Words:
What message would you give to would-be volunteers?
"I know that the kind of volunteer work I do might not be right for everyone. I brought a friend and co-worker once, and she didn't come back. She almost started crying. Sometimes when you see people in need, it's easier to not look at them; it's too painful. But there are always other ways that people can help. Manna House also has a clothing ministry. This co-worker now organizes our office to collect the clothes and shoes that people donate."

"I've learned that people will forget what you said, people will forget what you did, but people will never forget how you made them feel."
— Maya Angelou

The Cause:
The Manna House Food Distribution Center is dedicated to caring for the needs of the poor and hungry as a cooperative effort that networks churches, businesses, and individuals. Because "man shall not live by bread alone," it addresses the spiritual needs of individuals and families and seeks to identify the underlying causes of poverty. Manna House operates under the auspices of The Rock Urban Outreach Center, an independent entity for community transformation, and works with Angel Food, a program that provides assistance to families that need supplemental resources on a monthly basis. An outreach to supply weekend food to needy students through local schools has also been established.

Learn more at **www.TheRockFWC.org**

Photo: Nicole Allen

When Angelina isn't working or volunteering, you'll find her at the movies, watching TV, gardening, or reading a good novel.

The Kordenbrock-Rider Family are visiting & playing games.

LOCATION: COVINGTON, KY
OCCUPATION: Jennifer (mom): commercial banker;
Andy (dad): truck driver;
Drew, Natalie & Caitlynne: high school students;
Chelsea: college student

WELCOME HOUSE KENTUCKY, ST. CHARLES CARE CENTER

TIME WITH THESE ORGANIZATIONS:
1 year, 8 years respectively

THEIR TIME COMMITMENT:
4 hours a month

THEIR ROUTINE:
first Thursday night of the month at Welcome House, usually one Wednesday or Thursday a month at St. Charles Care Center

Two nights every month, the Kordenbrock-Rider family—two busy parents and four teenagers—can be found all in the same place, doing the same thing: being of service to others. One Christmas, when the family realized how many gifts they had, Jennifer and Andy wanted to demonstrate generosity to their kids. For a month, they pondered doing community service together: "Can we commit six people to do this?" All four of their kids play extracurricular sports and have jobs. They've made it work; they all know they're going to be together the first Thursday and at least one other night every month.

Once a month, they go for Family Night at St. Charles Nursing Home. They bring the residents down from their rooms, serve food, and visit with them. At Welcome House, a shelter for homeless women and children, the family brings or makes dessert—sundaes, brownies or cookies—and they play games or make a craft with the women and children. They play board games, Jenga, and Uno; they make jewelry and other crafts.

Photo: Nicole Allen

Twice a month, their big family gets bigger, and, as families do, they share their jokes, their stories, their humor, and their love.

CHANGING THE WORLD ON A TUESDAY NIGHT

IN THEIR OWN WORDS:

What's a way that volunteering has impacted your life?

Jennifer: "It's made me realize there are a lot of people less fortunate than I am; it makes you realize how fortunate you are. Your problems seem much smaller."

Natalie: "It makes me thankful for what I have."

Drew: "I realize how good I have it and how others don't."

Caitlynne: "It makes me feel accomplished."

Chelsea: "I feel good about myself when I help others."

What is an impactful or special moment you've experienced volunteering?

Natalie: "The kids at Welcome House really look up to us as role models, and that makes me feel good."

Drew: "Every time we leave Welcome House, the kids don't want us to leave, and that makes me feel good."

Jennifer: "One time, there was a kid there, in the homeless shelter, who went to the same high school as our kids. It makes you realize it can happen pretty quickly, and it can happen to anyone."

What do you think volunteering together does for you as a family?

Jennifer: "It gets us together, six of us who have different lives and schedules. It's almost like a holiday. It's rare that we have dinners all together, but twice a month, we are all together for this."

Andy: "It's something for us to do as a family. It's a good lesson for the kids to see that they don't have it that bad, that they have a good life. That was the whole idea of wanting to do this with them: to let them know there are people out there who really do have hard times and can really use your help."

Caitlynne: "It brings us closer together."

Natalie: "It brings us together, and it's a break from our normal lives. There's no fighting."

Drew: "It strengthens our bond as a loving, caring family."

Chelsea: "It makes me proud of us."

What message would you give to would-be volunteers?

Jennifer: "Make time in your schedule. Do it just once a month; it's better than nothing at all. Whenever I volunteer at the nursing home or at Welcome House, I feel humbled that I helped someone out today. You get a good feeling inside knowing that you did something good for someone, and someone appreciated what you did."

THE CAUSES:

Welcome House collaborates with the community to provide a continuum of quality services for individuals and families who are either homeless or at risk of becoming homeless, in order to eradicate homelessness, foster stability, and promote a just society.

Learn more at **www.WelcomeHouseKY.org**

St. Charles Care Center, a 105-bed skilled nursing facility, offers residential care for geriatric patients, for those convalescing from injuries or acute illnesses, and for those who suffer from a terminal illness. Staffed by registered nurses, licensed practical nurses, certified nurse assistants, social workers, recreation therapists, and support staff, the Care Center is licensed as a Skilled Nursing Facility by the Commonwealth of Kentucky and dually certified for Medicare and Medicaid.

Learn more at **www.StCharlesCare.org**

Lisa is protecting the planet.

LOCATION: INDIO, CA
AGE: 43
FAMILY: married, mother of three (ages 3, 6, and 8)
OCCUPATION: full-time mom, helps manage husband's business

GREENPEACE

TIME WITH THIS ORGANIZATION:
2 years

HER TIME COMMITMENT:
5 – 6 hours per week, on average

Lisa gives 115 percent to everything she does, which is why she almost didn't get involved in the global warming effort. Not one to just dabble in an endeavor, she was concerned that she didn't have time, as a mother of three small children, to "go all in."

Photo: John DeMello

A friend in Virginia persistently talked about wanting to do something about global warming because of the profoundly adverse impact it was already having on her children's future. Lisa promised to distribute, at her son's preschool, information on reducing one's carbon footprint if her friend sent her the fliers. Given her characteristic drive—and a background in journalism—the flier distribution evolved into much more. Lisa organized an Earth Day project whereby the preschool community made posters and distributed compact fluorescent bulbs, donated by Home Depot, along with information on how to be more environmentally responsible. She did a little PR, and the local television stations covered the event.

Lisa was "in." She began attending the meetings of The Coachella Valley Association of Governments Energy Conservation Subcommittee. And, having learned about the U.S. Mayors Climate Protection Agreement,

CHANGING THE WORLD ON A TUESDAY NIGHT

signed by 900+ cities to reduce their greenhouse gases to meet or beat standards outlined by the Kyoto Protocol, she figured she could launch a local city-by-city effort—a small-scale letter-writing campaign and visits to city council meetings to educate about the impacts of climate change. One city agreed, and another signed on after she worked with a city councilperson to bring in sixty local high-school students to talk about why finding a solution to global warming was critical to their future.

Lisa is a strong believer in doing one's research and developing a compelling argument. She likens her role to that of a used-car salesperson, "except, instead of cars, I'm selling the idea of a sustainable future."

When Greenpeace field organizer Eva Erbskorn spoke locally, Lisa saw that working with her to help influence federal legislation would create farther-reaching outcomes than any effort to reduce carbon emissions at the local level.

Lisa's primary motivation is her kids. "I want to do everything in my power to give them the best possible world, and the path we're on now isn't a very good one. That knowledge haunts me because they're going to have to live by the very wise or regrettable decisions we adults make."

Not only are Lisa's volunteer efforts good for the planet: she has grown as a public speaker, she is more organized and diplomatic, and she better understands human psychology and how to motivate others—starting with her kids. "They'll turn off lights when we leave a room. They understand what renewable energy is and why burning coal and oil is so devastating to the planet. They enjoy participating in rallies and marches and just being engaged. Hopefully I'm raising people who will be knowledgeable and responsible and active in their communities and their world."

In Her Own Words:

What's a way that volunteering has impacted your life?
"Not only does it bring meaning to life, it's my responsibility. By sheer luck, I was born in one of the wealthiest nations in the world. That's a privilege, and privilege should be recognized by volunteerism. It's easy to get caught up in the minutiae of everyday living, or in status and pleasure, but those things rob us of our humanity and an opportunity to glimpse the sublime. You get those things from getting over yourself and going beyond yourself and focusing on things that really matter and make a difference."

What message would you give would-be volunteers?
"We don't have to change the world. We can find joy and fulfillment in simply doing our part to help others or improve conditions in our communities. We can do what we can do, with our availability and skill set, to make a difference that collectively has a positive impact."

The Cause:

Greenpeace combines hard-hitting campaigns, powerful grassroots organizing, courageous direct action, and creative communications to win big victories for the environment. With a presence in forty countries, a fleet of four ships, and thousands of staff worldwide, it's one of the world's biggest and most effective environmental organizations. In the face of the accelerating, worldwide threat of global warming, Greenpeace is now building support for national and international action to solve this crisis once and for all.

Learn more at **www.ProjectHotSeat.org**

When Lisa isn't running her household or volunteering, you'll find her catching a movie, reading a book, or enjoying good food.

Brooks is preserving ecological diversity.

LOCATION: HILO, HI
AGE: 39
OCCUPATION: electronics technician, Smithsonian Observatory on Mauna Kea

THE NATURE CONSERVANCY

TIME WITH THIS ORGANIZATION:
3 years

HIS TIME COMMITMENT:
7 hours per month

HIS ROUTINE:
one Saturday per month, 8:30 am – 3:30 pm

Photo: John De Mello

Growing up in Minnesota, Brooks loved to explore the forest land right outside his back door. Once he was home from school, he'd bolt out the door to inspect bugs, scout out the best trees for climbing, and pick up rocks that caught his eye. This was his playground—no asphalt, no jungle gyms, just the land. By the time he reached high school, however, his back-door view had become cluttered with bulldozers, construction trailers, engineers in hard hats. Soon after, he became aware of The Nature Conservancy (TNC) and their mission to acquire and preserve land in agriculturally significant areas.

Naturally drawn to the magnificent beauty of Hawaii, Brooks now works with the Smithsonian's telescopes on the summit of Mauna Kea, an inactive volcano on the Big Island. Wanting to see more of the island and to help support the protection of it, he sought out that organization he'd heard about in his youth. Immediately after submitting an inquiry at The Nature Conservancy's website, he received an invitation to an upcoming volunteer day on one of the three preserves that TNC maintains on the island.

CHANGING THE WORLD ON A TUESDAY NIGHT

Among his many activities with TNC, Brooks has weeded areas where native plants are struggling, built a greenhouse, and repaired fences to keep destructive pigs and sheep out. A typical volunteer project can be completed in the seven hours that volunteers work on one Saturday per month. Brooks has also taken on more ambitious expeditions, including surveys lasting two to five days to monitor the populations of endangered and native birds. The volunteers start at the top of the forest and trek down, counting birds every 130 meters—a tedious, usually solo task, in sometimes difficult terrain and conditions. Brooks loves being so directly involved in projects that protect the species that make the island so unique. Some of his contributions are immediately visible, like the native mint seedling he'd planted just three months earlier that had grown into a three-foot-tall tree, heavy with flowers. Literally and figuratively, Brooks is planting seeds that will bloom a better future for his island.

IN HIS OWN WORDS:

What advice would you give to would-be volunteers?
"It's hard to get started, to get connected to the thing you'd be interested in, but if it goes well, then it's very easy to keep with it. The stuff that I do, is the stuff I would want to be doing on my day off anyway. That's how it's been easy for me."

What's the biggest thing you've learned?
"Working with The Nature Conservancy I've had a lot of experiences that I wouldn't have been able to have and gone to places on the island I wouldn't have been able to go, I got connected with bird surveys and learned a lot of things. And it's interesting, I've learned a lot more about native species and ecology in the places I used to live, since I've moved here and gotten involved with this work."

THE CAUSE:

The Nature Conservancy works in all fifty states and thirty countries to preserve the earth's ecological diversity by protecting its land and waters. It uses the best available science, a creative spirit, a non-confrontational, pragmatic approach, and partnerships with indigenous communities, businesses, governments, multilateral institutions, and other nonprofits to craft innovative solutions to complex conservation problems, at scales that matter and in ways that will endure.

Learn more at **www.NatureConservancy.org**

When Brooks isn't working or volunteering, you'll find him outside exploring the island.

Several studies that keep track of adults over a longer period of time have found that those individuals who volunteer at the beginning of a study tend to have lower mortality rates at the end of the study, even when taking into account such factors as physical health, age, socioeconomic status and gender.

Source: nationalservice.gov

A civilization flourishes when people plant trees under which they will never sit

GREEK PROVERB

Jesse is searching & rescuing.

LOCATION: LAKE HAVASU CITY, AZ
AGE: 26
FAMILY: married, father of one (age, 4 months)
OCCUPATION: co-owner of a bottled-water and water-filtration company

MINUTEMAN CIVIL DEFENSE CORPS, SEARCH AND RESCUE TEAM

TIME WITH THIS ORGANIZATION:
2 years

HIS TIME COMMITMENT:
one long weekend per month

HIS ROUTINE:
a 6-hour drive to the border on Friday morning, returning home on Sunday night

Jesse really takes to heart the old adage "Believe what you see, not what you hear." Living in Arizona, a border state embroiled in the controversy over illegal immigration, he was exposed to, what he describes as, media reports insinuating that the Minuteman Civil Defense Corps (MCDC) was full of racist members out to harm immigrants entering the United States illegally. Curious to know if these allegations were true, Jesse got in his truck and drove the six hours down to the border to find out for himself. What he discovered were, in his words, compassionate, patriotic, concerned citizens respectfully contributing to a cause they were committed to: protecting their borders.

Jesse learned that the founder of the organization, Chris Simcox, had recently created a new division whose sole purpose is to conduct search-and-rescue campaigns in the desert and rugged mountains of southern Arizona for illegals who have been abandoned by their traveling companions or have become lost in the harsh elements. Inspired by this team's mission, Jesse joined immediately, completing their three-day intensive training and self-funding $450 in equipment and supplies. Setting out at night, working as long as 24 to 44 hours at a time, Jesse and his teammates comb the desert, from north to south, where people who appear lost

CHANGING THE WORLD ON A TUESDAY NIGHT

or alone have been spotted. Sometimes they sit on active trails, waiting and watching, and ask the groups coming through if anyone needs food, water, or medical help. They're not there to detain—that is not their role. They're just there to help.

"It only takes the average illegal three to four days to get from the southern border to Tucson," Jesse explains. "There isn't just one trail they take; there are hundreds if not thousands of trails coming in to the US from Mexico. Their journey isn't an easy one, but a dangerous hike up and over mountains, through 120°+ summer weather, not to mention freezing temperatures in the winter and wild animals. We've run across people who tell us they've been out there for five to ten days. If they've been out there that long, it's because they've been left by the "coyote," a person who smuggles them across into the US, or they are lost or were left behind. Those are the people we are looking for. None of the illegals in these groups are going to call the authorities if someone is missing or lost. They don't want to get into trouble so they leave it alone. No search is ever performed or started for these people who are lost. We run into dehydration during the summer, people who are lost and aren't equipped with enough water. In the winter, it's hypothermia because they didn't bring enough warm clothes."

Jesse knows that if we all expect that "someone else" will do it, no one will be the one to do it. Considering it his mission to save those who are out there waiting, one weekend per month he makes the long drive down the mountain, six hours to the border. He takes a day off from running his family-owned water-filtration business so that he can leave on Friday morning, returning on Sunday night. The search-and-rescue volunteers pay for their expenses—uniforms, fuel for travel to and from the border, food, lodging, medical gear—out of their own pockets.

Jesse frequently speaks about his work around his home state, hoping to change public perception about the attitudes and convictions of his fellow MCDC volunteers. He carries built-in credibility: his parents were born in Mexico and entered the US legally through adoption and marriage. Jesse is proud of his heritage and culture, and also proud of his affiliation with an organization that defends against what he believes are the dangers and risks, to both Americans and Mexicans, of illegal immigrants crossing over into this country.

In His Own Words:
What inspires you to volunteer?
"We save lives every time we go down there. It's a given that we'll pull out at least one person each time. I donate my time because it needs to be done. People are lost and they hope that someone will come along and save their life—that's why I do it."

The Cause:
The Minuteman Civil Defense Corps (MCDC) is a peaceful, law-abiding and citizen-led initiative organized to stand watch at our borders, report illegal activities to the proper authorities, and build border fencing on private lands using private donations. Additionally, MCDC seeks to urge local and federal officials to enforce our immigration laws in order to keep our families and country safe.

The MCDC Search & Rescue team was established for the sole purpose of conducting search and rescue missions in the border crossing area. Extensive training is required of each volunteer member, including becoming nationally certified in Search & Rescue, learning CPR, First Aid, and GPS navigation. Each member is required to carry 2 gallons of extra rescue water, and first aid kits to help any person they encounter in the desert.

Learn more at **www.MinutemanHQ.com**

When Jesse isn't working or volunteering, you'll find him gardening, catching a show with friends, or traveling with his wife.

Omar is building homes.

HABITAT FOR HUMANITY OF OMAHA

TIME WITH THIS ORGANIZATION:
2 ½ years

•

HIS TIME COMMITMENT:
10 hours per week

•

HIS ROUTINE:
Saturdays from 8:30 - 4:00 pm, and Thursdays from 5:30 pm "until we're done"

LOCATION: OMAHA, NE
AGE: 21
OCCUPATION: full-time college student; part-time VIP coordinator, Harrah's Casino

Photo: Tree DeAngelis

Omar lives in extremes. In addition to being a full-time college student, he works part-time as the VIP coordinator at Harrah's Casino. He sees to it that the high rollers get the free drinks, free rooms, and other perks that the hotel provides for them. He takes care of folks who apparently have a lot of cash to risk.

On Saturdays, Omar helps build first-time homes for impoverished families, working alongside them as they put in their equity hours to earn their home. Omar understands what's at stake for them: he comes from their same humble beginnings.

Two years ago, Omar's mom was approved to work toward a home of her own. A single mom, she raised Omar and his sister on her small salary from delivering the local newspaper. She easily met the income criterion, equal to between 30% and 50% of the local median. The family or individual must also have the ability to pay a mortgage with no interest and an extended term, and be willing and able to put in three hundred fifty hours of sweat equity, building houses for other recipients as well as for themselves. In full support

CHANGING THE WORLD ON A TUESDAY NIGHT

of his mom and her dream, Omar showed up Saturday after Saturday, from early morning until late afternoon, and learned on the job about construction from the experts around him.

In the beginning, Omar was amazed by the numbers and types of people who showed up weekly to work on houses for perfect strangers. He imagined that those middle-class citizens had more important or fun things to do with their time. He really couldn't understand what compelled them to give their time, week after week.

Soon after his mom was accepted into the program, Omar became curious about the selection process. He learned that a committee comprising volunteers along with a paid staff member did the research used to decide who would be accepted and who wouldn't. Inspired, he decided he wanted to be a part of that process. Now an official member of the selection committee, Omar helps review hundreds of applications each Thursday evening, interview potential recipients, and visit them in their current places of residence. The committee then convenes and recommends to the board who they believe are most deserving and qualified to be accepted into the program. And though his mom's equity hours have been fulfilled, Omar keeps showing up on Saturdays anyway. He now understands why "perfect strangers" come back week after week.

"I will never forget that in no other country on Earth is my story even possible."
— President Barack Obama

In His Own Words:
What's a way that volunteering has impacted your life?
"I got to see all the aspects of volunteering, and that has influenced me to want to pursue a career in, or work closely with, a nonprofit. The power of volunteer work is just amazing. I didn't know it was that beneficial. It has helped a lot of communities and has helped me and my family personally. I love to see families when they get their house. That makes all the hard work worth it."

The Cause:
Habitat for Humanity of Omaha was established in 1984, after a small group of community members grew concerned about substandard living conditions in the city. Their founding mission—"Building homes and building lives through the partnership of our community's spiritual and material resources"—continues to guide the organization more than two decades and two hundred fifty homes later. To celebrate its twenty-fifth anniversary, Habitat for Humanity aims to complete twenty-five more homes in partnership with families and supporters throughout the city.

Learn more at
www.Habitat.org

Photo: Tree DeAngelis

When Omar isn't working or volunteering, you'll find him studying for school, spending time with his girlfriend, playing tennis, watching movies, or going for a swim.

Alisha is preparing for disasters.

Location: Mission, KS
AGE: 26
FAMILY: married
OCCUPATION: emergency services technology, program assistant

MEDICAL RESERVE CORPS

TIME WITH THIS ORGANIZATION:
3 years

HER TIME COMMITMENT:
10 – 20 hours a month

Alisha remembers being pulled in a little red wagon by her mother as she marched with a group of women, all holding signs. A toddler, she couldn't read the signs but recalls her mother's pin with a broken coat hanger on it. She remembers elementary school classmates saying they'd seen her mom on TV, telling people to "vote no on prop-something." When she learned that her mother was a lobbyist for reproductive rights, she knew only that it involved stuffing lots of envelopes and leaving messages on people's answering machines. As it turns out, her mother also sat on the board of Planned Parenthood for several years.

Photo: Megan Barnes

Alisha's grandfather told his granddaughter, that the true measure of someone's character is their ability to fight for other people's rights—rights that they themselves may never have to demand. Legally blind, he fought hard for the blind community's rights, eventually making his way to the Kansas State House of Representatives, where he worked to enact legislation that protected civil liberties. With two powerful leaders of service in her family, Alisha was taught at an early age that she must leave the world better than how she found it; how she would accomplish that was up to her.

A few years ago, searching on VolunteerMatch.org for an opportunity that inspired her, Alisha found a posting by the Medical Reserve Corps (MRC), a network of

CHANGING THE WORLD ON A TUESDAY NIGHT

medical and non-medical volunteers who support regional public health initiatives in times of community need. She had an interest in emergency medicine and was taking First Responder courses, so it seemed like a good fit. When Hurricane Katrina hit mid-semester, she wanted to jump in her car and head down to Louisiana: "You know that feeling when something awful happens and someone tells you, 'It's going to be okay'? Even though you know the road ahead isn't an easy one, there's something instinctively comforting about going through it with someone at your side. That feeling, that security,—I really wanted to give that to others."

Alisha admits she'd been concerned that she wouldn't be qualified for MRC, that the doctors and nurses would look down on her because she hadn't completed any medical training. She soon learned that volunteers with no medical experience fill important roles: updating the volunteer database, staffing outreach booths, and even providing hand-washing presentations for elementary students. Alisha explains, "Some tasks take only twenty minutes a week, but a lot of twenty-minute tasks can pile up. Logistics are a big part of our mission. Fifty percent of our volunteers don't have medical training, and they don't really need to; not every member of my unit is interested in being deployed." Alisha, however, did go on to complete her First Responder program and emergency medical technician (EMT) certification training that following spring.

Like her mother and grandfather, Alisha feels called to volunteer, as her duty to humankind: "I'm really inspired by the brevity of life. If this short eightyish years we have on this planet is all we ever get, I'd really like to make the best of it. A primary theme in my daily life is my belief that it's up to me to actively seek justice and work to protect my community. Ultimately, we all have to think like that. If we all assume someone else will do it, nothing will ever get done. So, one by one, we lend our voices to this greater cause, and what starts as a whisper becomes a roar for something larger than ourselves."

"Go out into the world and do well, but more importantly, go out into the world and do good."
— *Minor Myers, Jr.*

In Her Own Words:

What's a way that volunteering has impacted your life?
"It's a really good moral compass. I'm learning a lot about myself, probably most significantly, to be patient. A lot of disaster preparedness is waiting; you rush to get the training and then you wait and hope you never have to use it."

What message would you give to would-be volunteers?
"Don't be intimidated by the initial process; you will find your place in no time. Don't worry about not being trained; if you need training, your organization can point you in the right direction. Time is the greatest gift you can ever give; even if you don't have money or assets, you always have time—and I tend to think that a gift of time is more meaningful."

The Cause:

The Medical Reserve Corps of Greater Kansas City (MRCKC) is a network of medical and non-medical volunteers who support regional public health initiatives in times of need. Through their partnerships with public health, emergency management, and other volunteer entities, MRCKC serves a regional population of over two million people. Its volunteers promote healthy resilient communities through education outreach, participation in emergency preparedness exercises, vaccine distribution, and special-need sheltering.

Learn more at **www.MedicalReserveCorps.gov**

When Alisha isn't working or volunteering, you'll find her finishing up a degree in emergency management, checking out an art exhibit, or attending a local lecture.

Linda is mentoring via webcam.

LOCATION: PITTSBURGH, PA
AGE: 53
FAMILY: married, mother of three (ages 13, 18, and 21)
OCCUPATION: substitute teacher

INFINITE FAMILY

TIME WITH THIS ORGANIZATION:
over 1 year

HER TIME COMMITMENT:
2 hours per week

HER ROUTINE:
Fridays at 7:30 am, from her home computer

A computer powers up and a family logs on in Pittsburgh, Pennsylvania. At the same time, an orphaned teenager logs on at a computer lab in sub-Saharan Africa. Through the miracle of the Internet and web cameras with built-in microphones, Linda, a "Video Mentor," and her family, connect with their "Net Buddy," Tumi, through a program created by Infinite Family.

Thousands of African children are orphaned every year by AIDS, usually left to fend for themselves, care for younger siblings, and sort out life's challenges. The ratio of children to available adults in many areas is 12 to 1. Infinite Family has created an internet mentoring program that allows adults

Photo: Richard Schultz

CHANGING THE WORLD ON A TUESDAY NIGHT

and families all over the world to provide love, friendship, and guidance to these parentless children thousands of miles away.

Linda learned about Infinite Family from Dana Gold, a fellow church member who is a program director with the organization. Her three kids and husband were as excited as she was to jump in—so it really is a family affair!

Fifteen-year-old Tumi lost her parents to AIDS when she was young. The computer lab where she connects with her Net Family is at a local orphanage, but she doesn't live there. She lives in an informal settlement on local farm land, and walks nearly a mile to school and another half mile to get to the computer lab, a distance she walks on Saturday mornings, too, when she has her second call with her Net Family.

Tumi excitedly talks about school and boys and cars with Linda's daughter, also a teenager, and her son and Tumi share websites and draw things on the Infinite Family's website whiteboard. And, as Linda says, "They just giggle. It's so funny. All the barriers of being in a different country and being a different age seem to melt away, and they are just kids having fun."

Linda talks with Tumi about her schoolwork and asks if she needs help with any math problems; Tumi and one of Linda's kids both take algebra, so they can help each other. Linda confesses, "She's a normal teenager and doesn't want to spend the time working on her homework."

When staff members of Infinite Family visited Africa, they were able to deliver to Tumi an envelope stuffed with photographs of Linda's family. In return, Tumi sent back, with the Infinite Family staff, a big envelope containing beaded necklaces for everyone, a keychain, cards she'd made, and pictures of her when she was little. "That just blows me away," Linda says, "because these kids are in no position to be giving gifts."

In Her Own Words:

What do you love about this opportunity?

"That we are actually having a relationship with Tumi, who is in South Africa! We have a one-on-one relationship with her, instead of just sending money or supplies. It's the ongoing relationship that's the magic of it."

What's a way that volunteering has impacted your life?

"It has carried me through my entire life. You can always volunteer no matter what stage of life you're in. Even more than any professional experience I've had, my volunteer experience has been the most rewarding. If you told me that when I was a kid, I wouldn't have believed it. Each time I've done anything as a volunteer, I've always gotten more out of it than I put in. Tumi has changed our life."

What message would you give to would-be volunteers?

"Don't hesitate; just jump in and do it. Don't be afraid. The most rewarding feeling is the sense of knowing that you accomplished something and made a difference in somebody else's life."

The Cause:

Infinite Family strengthens and inspires vulnerable southern African children to lead fulfilling lives by connecting them with caring mentors from around the world. Through video conferencing, email, and a secure internet platform, southern African children in orphanages and after-school programs come face-to-face with nurturing adults once a week for half-hour conversations. Children gain confidence in technology and hope for their future, and feel loved by a special adult who sets time aside each week just for them.

Learn more at **www.InfiniteFamily.org**

When Linda isn't working or volunteering, you'll find her spending time with her family, traveling, biking, swimming, or camping.

The Top Five Large Cities for Volunteer Rate:
1. Minneapolis-St. Paul, MN
2. Salt Lake City, UT
3. Austin, TX
4. Seattle, WA
5. Oklahoma City, OK

Source: volunteeringinamerica.gov

> Go Out and Do Something for Somebody. Go Out and Give Something to Somebody — it will take you away from yourself and make you happy.
>
> — Joseph Jefferson

Emily is raising puppies.

LOCATION: SANTA FE, NM
AGE: 50-something
FAMILY: married, mother of two (both in their 20s)
OCCUPATION: scientist

Their current jobs, with their long commutes, take Emily & her husband away from the house for at least twelve hours a day. This makes it challenging for them to own a dog, as they'd always done before moving to New Mexico. Wanting to do something with animals, therapeutic horses or dogs, Emily did an Internet search and discovered Assistance Dogs of the West (ADW).

ASSISTANCE DOGS OF THE WEST

TIME WITH THIS ORGANIZATION:
6 years

•

HER TIME COMMITMENT:
weekends & holidays

•

HER ROUTINE:
works with trainers on Thursday nights for about an hour, then takes the dog home for the weekend and holidays.

Photo: Spencer Wright

CHANGING THE WORLD ON A TUESDAY NIGHT

Assistance Dogs of the West matches clients with a dog trained for general assistance, seizure, psychiatric service, social therapy, or facility placement. ADW dogs are taught over ninety commands over a period of eighteen to twenty-four months. The primary job of a volunteer puppy raiser is to reinforce the skills the dog learns during its formal training and to teach it how to operate one-on-one in a home environment. The volunteer ideally attends the formal trainings with a trainer on Thursday nights, after which, the dog goes home with the volunteer through the weekend. (The dog also spends holidays with the volunteer.) On Monday mornings, the dog is either dropped off or picked up so it can resume its training at ADW's facility. During the week, the dogs also visit the local Montessori school, nursing homes, and hospitals.

Now raising her fifth ADW dog, Emily, along with her husband, thoroughly enjoys the journey of raising these dogs, but the real reward comes when they hear about their dogs' new homes from ADW staff. Sometimes they're lucky enough to receive detailed emails and photos from the new owners. Gus, a mellow, gallant yellow lab, helps a woman, with a disease that prohibits her from seeing below her waist, navigate inside and outside the home. Libby, an audacious, confident black lab, helps an autistic girl, who has gotten more involved in school activities, maintain a steadier state. Logan, an intrepid yellow lab, enlivens a graduate student, who has decreased his antidepressant medication and is now the captain of his lacrosse team, with Logan as the traveling team mascot. Gabe, a gutsy, self-assured yellow lab, assists a nineteen-year-old paraplegic who's entering his first year in college and wants to work independently after he graduates.

"Live as if you were to die tomorrow. Learn as if you were to live forever."
— Mohandas Gandhi

IN HER OWN WORDS:
What is a special moment you've experienced volunteering?
"I got to meet the person who was getting Gabe. Antonio is a young man who acquired the Hanta virus, a disease that's transferred from mice to humans, and he lost the use of his legs. He was full of energy and life; he'd already altered his truck so he could drive with his hands. It seems he'd passed the stage of mourning his loss and was looking towards the future. Antonio was so ready to work with a dog. Knowing Gabe, I knew the two of them would just click. Gabe is a 'guy's dog'; he's outgoing, and you'd never put him full-time under a desk. Antonio was earning a BS degree in forestry, and I can see Gabe sitting by his side in his pickup truck. They're a perfect fit. That's the payback you get for the small amount of time you put in."

What message would you give to would-be volunteers?
"You just have to take the plunge, get immersed, and find out about yourself. And, in doing so, you'll find what works. Find something you love."

THE CAUSE:
Assistance Dogs of the West was founded in 1995 with the core value of respect for the unique abilities of humans and animals. Every month, more than thirty potential clients call or email, expressing some feeling of being cut off or marginalized from the world around them. New owners become more independent and self-reliant, equipped with a "tool" for increased mobility and environmental safety, and more emotionally secure with nonjudgmental, loving companionship 24/7.

Learn more at **www.AssistanceDogsoftheWest.org**

When Emily isn't working or volunteering, you'll find her doing something outdoors, usually with her family and/or dogs (hiking, backpacking, snowshoeing, cross-country skiing, or motorcycle riding).

Olga is creating possibilities.

LOCATION: CHANHASSEN, MN
AGE: 32
OCCUPATION: architectural designer

BRIDGE BUILDERS FOR KIDS

TIME WITH THIS ORGANIZATION:
just over a year

•

HER TIME COMMITMENT:
2 hours a week

An architectural designer might be involved in building bridges, but the bridges that Olga builds connect not land masses but children to a more promising future. Passionate about kids, Olga has always volunteered in ways that serve them. When Bridge Builders for Kids (BBFK) announced in her church's weekly bulletin that they needed volunteers for summer camp, she sent them her resume. During the initial meeting to discuss the volunteer opportunities, she learned that BBFK mentors children of prisoners year-round for eight to thirteen years. Noting that Olga was currently unemployed, they offered her a part-time job, helping with administration management, finances,

CHANGING THE WORLD ON A TUESDAY NIGHT

event planning, and general office duties, in addition to summer-camp counseling. Not only did working for BBFK provide her with an outlet for her passion, it helped fill the gap while she was seeking full-time employment in her field.

Olga has since started her own property management & architectural design firm, working more than full-time, as many small-business owners do, but she continues volunteering with BBFK, doing much of the same work she did as a part-time employee. Her year with Bridge Builders has expanded her capacity to see people as individuals, minus the labels we immediately place on them: "I realize that there's always something else going on; it's not what we see at first. I see the beauty of these children and realize there's something great in everybody. When a child acts out, I see that child first, for who they are, and not their reaction to a situation."

Olga also recently completed training to become a Guardian Ad Litem (GAL) and Court Appointed Special Advocate for at risk children. The GAL speaks for the child's best interests in child-protection proceedings, following the case as it moves through the court system and making recommendations to the court as decisions are made that affect the child's well-being. With this new commitment, she'll be giving an additional five to ten hours per month in the service of children.

"Give, and it will be given to you. A good measure, pressed down, shaken together and running over, will be poured into your lap. For with the measure you use, it will be measured to you."

— Luke 6:38

In Her Own Words:
What's a way that volunteering has impacted your life?

"It's given me a broader perspective on life. It opens my mind and allows me to view a world beyond myself. When I haven't spent so much time giving back, my world seems minimized and I tend to complain more about my life. However, when I see other people's lives and the need they have, I remember how blessed my life is. It shows me that even though I'm not the richest person, I have a lot to give. It's amazing how little can make a difference for someone else. I get to learn so much from children: they're honest and the best teachers; they teach you things you didn't learn in school. I also enjoy meeting other volunteers and adults from all social-economic, racial, and cultural backgrounds. It enriches one's life."

The Cause:
Bridge Builders for Kids, a Christ-centered ministry, provides year-round support to children of prisoners through one-to-one mentoring and other relationship-building activities. Its preventive/proactive approach helps break the destructive cycle whereby seven out of ten children of prisoners enter the criminal justice system, by reaching the kids when they're between five and ten years old and offering support until they're eighteen. Bridge Builders also helps connect their families to additional resources and support through partner organizations and local churches.

*Learn more at **www.BridgeBuilders.cc***

When Olga isn't working or volunteering, you'll find her biking, taking dance classes, entertaining friends, or cooking, mostly Indian, African, or multicultural food influenced by her birth country of Uganda.

Abby is mentoring an immigrant.

LOCATION: Chicago, IL
AGE: 28
OCCUPATION: learning and talent consultant, Blue Cross Blue Shield

Barbara Kingsolver's *The Poisonwood Bible* was the first of many stories set in or about Africa that inspired Abby's vision to go to Africa, to work there and address the issues she'd been learning so much about. How this would be possible with her career and a new relationship, she didn't know, but Mawi Asgedom's *Of Beetles and Angels* opened a door. When Abby read the author's bio, which says that he lives in Chicago and lists local places accepting donations to support refugees, she remembered that Dave Eggers' *What Is the What?* also mentions that many refugees relocate to Chicago.

PAN-AFRICAN ASSOCIATION

TIME WITH THIS ORGANIZATION:
1 year

HER TIME COMMITMENT:
2 - 3 hours per week

HER ROUTINE:
generally Wednesdays

Photo: Brandon Williams

CHANGING THE WORLD ON A TUESDAY NIGHT

It suddenly clicked: she didn't have to uproot her life and travel to Africa to make a difference with the African people. She could do that in her own backyard, right there in her own city. Searching the Internet for work with African refugees, she discovered the Pan-African Association, whose mission is to serve, empower, and promote the interests of refugees and immigrants of African descent and beyond.

Primarily interested in becoming a mentor, Abby was matched with Neima, a 24-year-old immigrant from Ethiopia. Meeting a couple of hours every week, the two women shared family pictures and stories, and Abby assessed Neima's English skills. Because Abby doesn't have a background in teaching English, she hasn't given Neima formal English instruction, but helps with verb tenses and vocabulary in her ESL (English as a Second Language) class homework.

Abby tries to make learning English fun. They've had outings to the grocery store, swapping their languages' words for assorted items. And one night, they made flashcards for objects in Abby's house, then moved outside, then went to get ice cream, all the while adding words. Abby also helps Neima do everyday life things, like fill out immigration forms for her husband, who still lives in Ethiopia. Neima still feels somewhat alone and misses her family in Ethiopia so Abby invites her to different Chicago events and places where she can learn about American culture and feel more at home. When they first met, Neima was very quiet; now, she sometimes leads the conversation, telling Abby about her culture, its food, its traditional dances, among other things. Having improved her English, she now holds a half-time job at a grocery store, though ultimately she wants to go to school to take photography classes, as she was involved with a photography business in Africa. Shortly after Neima had started her new job, she invited Abby to meet for coffee and dessert at a neighborhood café. When Neima paid the bill, Abby protested but Neima insisted, "I invited you and it's my first paycheck, so I want to treat you." Abby was touched by her generosity—and gratified that her mentoring helped Neima reclaim her sense of empowerment.

In Her Own Words:

What message would you give to would-be volunteers?
"As busy as you are, you're never too busy to volunteer. It takes you outside of yourself and helps you think about somebody else and their well-being. Focusing on someone else and their needs is a good thing."

What's a way that volunteering has impacted your life?
"I've shared with others that I feel like I have a new sister. It's really nice to see her face light up when we spend time together. It's great to see her coming out of her shell. There's a friendship bond there. I hope that Neima and I will always to be a part of each other's lives."

The Cause:

Since 2002, the Pan-African Association has been dedicated to helping African refugees and immigrants achieve self-reliance and successfully integrate into American society. Pan-African Association's life-affirming programs include health outreach, adjustment and education services, individual mentoring, job readiness training, citizenship programs, cultural programs, and workshops.

Learn more at **www.PanAfricanAssociation.org**

> "You're going to come across people in your life who will say all the right words at all the right times. But in the end, it's always their actions you should judge them by. It's actions, not words, that matter."
> — Nicholas Sparks

When Abby isn't working or volunteering, you'll find her reading a book-club selection, cooking, traveling, or spending time with family.

DRESS FOR SUCCESS

TIME WITH THIS ORGANIZATION:
4 years

HER TIME COMMITMENT:
4 hours per month

HER ROUTINE:
second Saturday of the month

Beth is dressing women.

LOCATION: CINCINNATI, OH
AGE: 32
FAMILY: married, mother of two (ages 1 and 3)
OCCUPATION: high school history teacher

Attending graduate school in New York City to become a history teacher, Beth became keenly aware of social injustices. She studied them in her history books, in her classes, and saw them everyday on the streets beyond the classroom.

"It was the first time I'd related the history of our society to contemporary life in a meaningful way, and I was moved like I hadn't ever been moved before. Living in the city awakened something in me where I finally saw these issues I'd been studying—racial and class stratification, immigration, gender equity—as more than just abstract topics for an abstract seminar. I began to see these issues in more personal, and less academic, ways. For example, I focused on slavery and abolitionism in my graduate work. Through that study, I began to recognize the bravery and the fortitude it took to stand up for something that was right, even in the face of massive resistance, and I understood the legacy that something like slavery leaves in our culture. It was this combination—my desire to emulate those who

Photo: Nicole Jones

CHANGING THE WORLD ON A TUESDAY NIGHT

went before me in doing what's right and my feeling that history affects people in our society, some positively and some negatively—that led me to volunteer." Beth relates.

It was the Lenten holiday eight years ago that prompted Beth to take action and find an organization to volunteer with. Instead of the customary "giving something up," she wanted to give something to someone who needed it: her time.

New to Cincinnati, she joined the Junior League because it was a good way to get exposed to lots of different opportunities. During her two years with them, one of their projects was an event for Dress for Success Cincinnati (DFSC) which provides career clothing and counseling for women in transition. Connecting with their cause immediately, Beth decided to directly volunteer with DFSC.

On the 2nd Saturday of every month, Beth gives up pancakes and cartoons with her family to volunteer for the DFSC suiting events. Ten to twenty-five women show up at the Dress for Success "store"—a retail-type space fully stocked with women's clothing, shoes, and accessories that have been donated by local residents and organizations. Five to twelve volunteers work like personal shoppers to help select a flattering interview ensemble for each woman.

"By the end of a session," Beth says, "our clients always come out looking fabulous and feeling pretty good, too. If you're lucky, you develop a rapport with each client while you're with them, which makes it easier to talk about upcoming interviews. My hope is that chatting with them about what to expect from the interviews alleviates some of their anxiety. And I love that DFSC offers classes on everything from résumé writing to interview preparation to financial literacy. It's not just about the outfit, but that's a great start. When people feel good about how they look, it empowers them to go further in their life. Some of their personal stories are the stuff of nightmares: physical, mental, and chemical abuse, criminal backgrounds, etc. Each client's story is different, but the common thread is their desire to pick themselves up and move on. Dress for Success helps them help themselves to achieve, and that doesn't feel like charity; it feels like a stepping stone."

DFSC works with women, referred from social service agencies, who have recently come out of rehab, battered women's shelters, or prison, and wish to find a job. Dress for Success professionally suits them for their first week of work for free.

A typical middle-class, successful woman, Beth was concerned that she wouldn't be able to make genuine connections with the women she was serving, that they wouldn't feel she could relate to them. She has been surprised and gratified that these courageous women don't care at all about their differences and are willing to open up and share with her.

In Her Own Words:
What message would you give would-be volunteers?
"If you're going to volunteer, you should look for opportunities that matter to you. And be sure to connect what matters to you to your community service project. Finding the right community service program is kind of like dating. You may have to try several different organizations to find 'The One.'"

The Cause:
Dress for Success Cincinnati is one of 113 affiliates around the world that provides free interview attire to women seeking employment toward self-sufficiency. Volunteers work one-on-one with the women to find the right professional look—clothing, shoes, jewelry, handbag—to ensure a good first impression and make them feel empowered to land the job.

Learn more at **www.DressforSuccess.org**

When Beth isn't working or volunteering, you'll find her reading, walking in the neighborhood, paying attention to politics, or spending time with her family.

44 percent of adults volunteer. That means 83.9 million American adults volunteer, representing the equivalent of over 9 million full-time employees at a value of $239 billion.

Source: IndependentSector.org

Kindness
is the language which the deaf can hear and the blind can see.

MARK TWAIN

StandUp for Kids

TIME WITH THIS ORGANIZATION:
2 years

HER TIME COMMITMENT:
3 – 9 hours per week

HER ROUTINE:
*Thursdays
5:30 – 8:30 pm*

Allison is setting an example.

Location: Oceanside, CA
AGE: 32
FAMILY: mother of two (ages 9 and 15)
OCCUPATION: nuclear oversight supervisor, San Onofrea Nuclear Power Plant

Allison's life today is a long way from her life on the streets of Oceanside as a pregnant teen. Now she volunteers her time to mentor teens whose shoes she walked in. She knows firsthand what that existence is like, what resources are and are not available, what challenges these kids face as they try to stabilize their life and create a future for themselves. Allison met her former husband on the streets, where he was also living at the time, and together they rebuilt their lives and created a family.

A busy mom and also a volunteer on two advisory groups for the City of Oceanside, Allison donates her time at a shelter operated by StandUp for Kids. Every Thursday night—and other nights when she has the time—she serves as a resource and role model for homeless teens or at-risk kids living in homes unsuitable for their growth and development. She helps them identify resources, complete paperwork for medical care, and participates in activities as simple as playing games, cooking and eating together, and just being there as a caring adult. Fifteen to forty kids show up at the shelter on any given night.

CHANGING THE WORLD ON A TUESDAY NIGHT

Allison provides kind support—and hope: her great life demonstrates what's possible after life on the streets. Kids end up without a home for a wide variety of reasons, but being understood by someone who's been there is a powerful motivator for leaving their past behind them and creating the life they want.

"We make a living by what we get, but we make a life by what we give."
— Winston Churchill

In Her Own Words:

What inspires you to volunteer?
"It's just kind of been in my nature to help others; it makes you feel good. Charity work is an important aspect in life to keep you happy, make others happy, and keep you humble. I also do it to be an example to my children; they come with me to volunteer when they can."

What's a way that volunteering has impacted your life?
"It's made me a lot happier; it brings joy in my life. It's kind of a karma thing: a lot of good things happen to me because I do good. I also love to see someone affected in a positive way by my guidance."

What's message would you give to would-be volunteers?
"There's got to be, in a month's time, a few hours that you can fit in somewhere. Try it out once. If you don't like it, fine. But it will be pretty impossible to not like it. Someone will touch your heart and make you feel good."

The Cause:

StandUp For Kids helps homeless and street kids in cities and towns across America, by providing street outreach counseling, transitional living, and outreach centers with meals and snacks, showers, laundry, clothing, hygiene products, educational assistance, referral services, and telephone-message and mail service. Volunteer-driven, each StandUp For Kids chapter creates a safe and protective, real-home environment so the kids know they're cared for and can stabilize their lives.

Learn more at **www.StandUpForKids.org**

Photo: Robert Weeks

When Allison isn't working or volunteering, you'll find her with her son's Cub Scout pack, taking her daughter to the girl's church group, or at home with her kids, watching movies and playing games.

Lisa is giving music.

Location: Las Vegas, NV
AGE: 45
OCCUPATION: church pianist/organist, private piano teacher

Music is Lisa's life. She's the band music director at her church; she teaches private piano lessons; she's the former president of the Las Vegas Music Teachers Association (LVMTA).

Photo: James Tanksley

Under Lisa's leadership, the LVMTA created and delivered its annual Playathon, a series of Christmas recitals at local malls to generate funds for a different charity every year. After eight years in this role, Lisa wanted to move on, to volunteer her musical skills and passion elsewhere, though where, she didn't know.

While stopped at an intersection one day, Lisa got her "Eureka!" when a blind girl with a cane crossed the street right in front of her car. She was moved to tears as she realized that people who can't see, who have a heightened sense of hearing, would be inspired to create music. Discovering The Blind Center of Nevada in the phone book, she called to inquire about volunteering in their music department. But they didn't have a music program!

Six months went by before Lisa called again; she just wasn't sure what she could do since they didn't have a music program in place. Again, the woman who answered the phone invited her to visit. And this time, she did.

THE BLIND CENTER OF NEVADA

TIME WITH THIS ORGANIZATION:
4 years

HER TIME COMMITMENT:
3 – 5 hours per week

HER ROUTINE:
Friday afternoon lessons and email coordination from home

Changing the World on a Tuesday Night

That's how the music program at The Blind Center of Nevada got started, from one phone call and the courage to call again and explore the possibilities. Lisa contacted local music teachers to see if they wanted to volunteer there, too. But before they could teach any lessons, they needed instruments, so the music teachers came together to raise funds. Keyboards were the first to arrive, and students began learning piano. Then a grand piano was donated, and a fiddle club donated five violins and recruited a violin teacher for the program. After finding a piano teacher who also teaches harp, they raised money through the LVMTA Playathon to purchase a harp.

The program now includes a piano-tuning course. Its instructor drives two hours each way, twice a week, to teach two adults who want to learn it as a trade. The community strives to add one new component each year; last year, it was a choir teacher. And recently, a big music room—home for the music program—was added when The Blind Center received grant money to expand their facility.

Lisa hears story after story about the mainstream educational system's failure to teach music to blind or visually impaired children, primarily because of the misconception that they can only learn music by Braille, and secondarily, because it takes additional time to employ recording devices.

"I was teaching a young woman piano, and I asked her if she took any music classes in school. She said she was really interested in learning clarinet, but her teacher couldn't help her. I found a clarinet at Goodwill and a teacher who was willing to come in and teach her, all within just a couple of weeks. She's playing beautifully now. She also now has a job and is living independently. Having a hobby and a skill lifts people up; it increases their self-esteem."

The Blind Center's music program has been developing methods for school music teachers to instruct blind and visually impaired children. The teacher speaks the music, note by note, into a recording device, and the students learn it by memory. Lisa aims to create a course to share with teachers worldwide, based on the methods they've been developing at The Blind Center of Nevada.

In Her Own Words:
What message would you give would-be volunteers?
"Being a volunteer means giving of yourself without expecting any return whatsoever. We get so caught up in that cynical human formula—'What do I get out of it?'—that you really feel your life has purpose when you give selflessly in such a way. I know a few people who traded high salaries for lower-paying jobs just so they feel they're contributing something positive to the world. It's hard to know why humans are this way, but I think we all feel compassion for the less fortunate and wish there was a way to help. Volunteering for a good cause gives your life purpose."

The Cause:
The Blind Center of Nevada provides a positive social setting and support system outside the home for individuals who are blind or visually impaired. For many, its work opportunities, programs, social activities, and services have become a way of life: transportation, computer classes, independent living skills training, Braille instruction, arts and crafts, bowling, day trips (e.g., shopping, fishing, picnics), dinners, dances, and a job training center.

Learn more at **www.BlindCenter.org**

"Kindness is a language which the deaf can hear and the blind can see."
— Mark Twain

When Lisa isn't working or volunteering, you'll find her rehearsing music with one of her bands.

RESPECT International

TIME WITH THIS ORGANIZATION:
6 years

HER TIME COMMITMENT:
4 - 6 hours per week

HER ROUTINE:
most weekends and some weekday evenings before her husband and son arrive home

Sandrine is translating.

Location: Edison, NJ

AGE: 38

FAMILY: married, mother of one (age 2)

OCCUPATION: copywriter for international publishing company

Photo: Anthony Saint James

In a refugee camp in Africa, a bright spot in a kid's day is receiving a pen-pal letter from a non-refugee student in another part of the world. No e-mails or text messages, but handwritten, personal letters sharing thoughts, questions and ideas are sent between children who live worlds apart.

As the French Coordinator for RESPECT International, Sandrine makes sure those connections get made, using her French language skills and a few spare hours in her week. Sandrine receives all of the requests for pen pals that are sent in from French-speaking refugee children. She reviews the requests to make sure that they meet the criteria of the program and then works with French-speaking schools in Canada, Europe and the United States to find students who are interested in connecting through the letter exchange program. A big map hangs in Sandrine's home, where she does her volunteer work, allowing her to pinpoint all of the locations she's connecting, on three continents.

When Sandrine moved from France to the United States, she wanted to volunteer here, as

CHANGING THE WORLD ON A TUESDAY NIGHT

she'd done in France—and as did her grandmother, who'd handwritten letters for Amnesty International. Browsing the internet, she chanced upon an opening at RESPECT International. Sandrine feels it's her role to connect people: "Connection is important. We can understand people better and find out each one's needs and goals. It's not only what's inside the letters that matters but also the fact that people connect with each other. Receiving one letter from another country, from someone so far away who cares for them, is an amazing adventure for the students from Europe and America, and even more so for isolated refugees in Africa."

Sandrine feels rewarded for her work every time she receives an email from a teacher in Africa saying that the letters "give [the kids] their smiles back." Teachers have told her that they feel the pen-pal program plays a part in the students' good results on their year-end exam. "They have a lot of gratitude," she notes.

Sandrine also gets involved in any other RESPECT International projects that can utilize her French language skills, usually in a liaison role. She's helped to organize computer shipping to Africa, and currently is working on a program that raises money to send books to schools in Africa. She's particularly proud of a project where she and a team of others organized, from their home computers, a training on HIV in Africa. They connected with contacts via email and organized an entire year long trip for the training volunteers. Sandrine marvels at how much can be accomplished by a small but committed group of people, using technology, working from home, with just a few hours of their time each week.

"I prefer to be a dreamer among the humblest, with visions to be realized, than lord among those without dreams and desires."
— Kahlil Gibran

In Her Own Words:
What does volunteering add to your life?
"I feel useful; for me, it's a goal. It's good to feel you're changing the world. We revive hope. We can do only small things, but if it's for one kid to recover hope, even if it's only one, it's tremendous. Now that I have my son, I want to help the kids even more."

What message would you give to would-be volunteers?
"You don't need a lot of time; you can do something even if you have only one hour on the weekend. It's up to you what you can do. You'll discover that you can make a difference, and you may develop an unknown talent. You just feel good because you feel useful for other people. It's for your ego, in a way; I wouldn't do it if I didn't have any pleasure in doing it. I'm not an exceptional person; I'm a really simple person."

The Cause:
RESPECT International, headquartered in Winnipeg, Manitoba, Canada, builds bridges between non-refugee and refugee students through a global pen-pal letter-exchange program that increases awareness of refugee issues among the non-refugee students. All the students learn about another culture and geography, and the non-refugee schools are encouraged to raise funds for their refugee school.

Learn more at **www.RespectRefugees.org**

When Sandrine isn't working or volunteering, you'll find her running, spending time with her husband and son, sharing a good dinner with friends, or attending a hockey game.

Africa is interpreting for patients.

LOCATION: Iowa City, IA
AGE: 30
OCCUPATION: environmental engineer

IOWA CITY FREE MEDICAL CLINIC

TIME WITH THIS ORGANIZATION:
4 years

•

HER TIME COMMITMENT:
5 - 6 hours per month

•

HER ROUTINE:
*Thursdays
6:15 - 9:30 pm,
once or twice a month*

Photo: Dawn Frary

When Africa's family immigrated to the United States from Chile for her father's education, the Iowa City Free Medical Clinic was essentially their family doctor for years. Africa remembers feeling embarrassed to go there, perhaps because the facilities weren't very modern at that time, the exam areas were separated by only a curtain, and even basic items like cough syrup were in short supply.

After completing her undergraduate degree in engineering, Africa returned to Iowa City to begin her career and build her life, but she wanted something more. She realized that she wanted to make a difference in her community. When she learned that the Free Medical Clinic needed volunteer Spanish interpreters, she knew it was the perfect place for her to give back—the place that had given so much to her.

Africa says, "It's so nice to see that it's changed to what it is today. They have an eye clinic, chronic care, a much larger pharmacy. They have dentists that come in now, too." As

CHANGING THE WORLD ON A TUESDAY NIGHT

an interpreter, she listens to Spanish-speaking patients discuss their ailments, describes the situation to the doctor or patient guide in English, and asks follow-up questions in Spanish as needed. She also helps with answering simple questions at the front desk, lab, and pharmacy.

Africa particularly recalls an elderly lady at the eye clinic, who couldn't read, not because of her failing vision, but because she didn't know how. As Africa helped the doctor strategize a creative solution for testing her in lieu of the standard reading test, she relayed the entire conversation to the woman. She was moved by how sweet and grateful the woman was, how reminiscent she was of Africa's grandmother.

"I know that I know nothing."
— Socrates

In Her Own Words:
What do you think keeps people from volunteering?
"They don't really know what the experience is like. If they took the initial step, they'd realize how great it is. Making the time to do it may be the most difficult, but if they did, they'd understand just how wonderful it is and how easy it is to regularly volunteer in your life."

What's a way that volunteering has impacted your life?
"At first, I thought it was going to be an arduous task, but it can be fun, and I actually look forward to my volunteering time. There's satisfaction in seeing how Spanish-speaking patients are so happy that someone can understand them and help them. They thank you so much. A lot of patients have old, supernatural beliefs; they want to know if something is wrong with their blood. It's good when they can get assurance that it's nothing like that."

The Cause:
The Iowa City Free Medical Clinic & Dick Parrott Free Dental Clinic (FMC/FDC) was founded in 1971 on the belief that health care is a basic human right. The FMC/FDC currently provides a wide range of acute and chronic outpatient medical care to the uninsured and underserved in Iowa City and the surrounding community. Committed to patient rights, including the right to privacy and confidentiality and to receive medical care without moral or social judgment, the clinic provides care at no cost, within the constraints imposed by available resources and the use of volunteers.

Learn more at **www.FreeMedicalClinic.org**

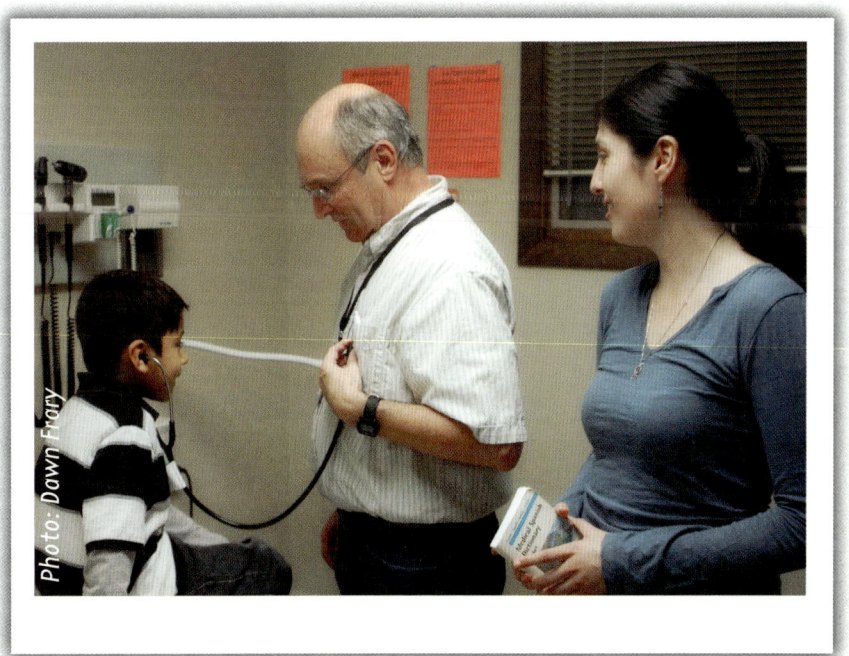

When Africa isn't working or volunteering, you'll find her playing the violin in the Iowa City Community String Orchestra or out for a run.

On average, Baby Boomers have the highest volunteer rate at 31.2%. The average volunteer rate for young adults ages 16-24 years is 22.3%, for college students it's 27.4%, and for adults ages 65 and older it's 24.2%.
Source: volunteeringinamerica.gov

Steve is cuddling babies.

Location: Manheim, PA
Age: 50
Occupation: vice president and trust officer, regional bank

An Arthur Frommer's magazine article first alerted Steven to the concept of volunteer vacations. Inspired by the opportunity to make a difference while traveling and unwinding on his annual two-week vacation, he looked into its programs. Little did he expect that his daily life would change, too.

In the late 80s, Steven was volunteering for a week at a time with several organizations traveling to Haiti, Honduras, and Nicaragua. During one of his Haiti trips, he happened to spend several hours at an orphanage maintained by Sisters of Charity in the capital city of Port-au-Prince. Walking from crib to crib, he held as many babies as he could, for as long as he could, trying to cover the four rooms, each housing fifty cribs.

On the flight home, Steven realized he could do something similar in his own country. In December 1990, he started volunteering one night a week at the Children's Hospital of Philadelphia, holding babies or spending time with sick kids. Several years later, deciding he could give more than one evening per week of his time, he began visiting the

Children's Hospital of Philadelphia, Penn State Children's Hospital, Global Volunteers

TIME WITH THESE ORGANIZATIONS:
18 years, 17 years, 10 years, respectively

HIS TIME COMMITMENT:
12 – 24 hours per week

HIS ROUTINE:
3 nights a week and a 2-week volunteer vacation

CHANGING THE WORLD ON A TUESDAY NIGHT

children at Penn State Children's Hospital, one night of the week initially, then eventually two.

In 1999, Steven learned about Global Volunteers' program working with children in an understaffed "failure to thrive" clinic in Romania—another one of those things that just felt like the right thing for him to do. That year, he took his first trip to Romania, and has been returning every September since, spending two weeks of his vacation time doing what parents normally do for their children: hold them, play with them, feed them, change their diapers.

Steven has seen firsthand the impact of volunteers and their love: "In 1999, I was on one of the first teams to go to Romania with Global Volunteers. At the time, in many orphanages, the babies would just lie there quietly in their cribs; they wouldn't even cry, because they knew they wouldn't get a response. The older children would, literally, bang their little heads against the walls. Throughout the years, with Global Volunteers continually sending teams over, I've witnessed these environments totally transform before my eyes. The babies are now in more normal conditions at this clinic; they cry and interact as children would who know that someone will hear their cry and respond. This is a direct result of their now being so used to having people around."

"To the world you might just be one person, but to one person, you just might be the world."
—Josephine Billings

IN HIS OWN WORDS:
What's a way that volunteering impacted your life?

"When you're doing something you love doing, it's like being with friends. The children give more to me than I can give to them. I so look forward to the time of the week when I can get out of the office and get to the hospital. I feel I'm making a difference in an important way; I feel satisfied, fulfilled, and relaxed there. I try to put myself in the children's place, thinking, 'What would I want if I were the patient?' Some long-term patients recognize me when I come in, and I've created some lasting relationships and memories."

THE CAUSES:

"Volunteers supply their special human connection—a connection of spirits that transcends miles of IV tubing and the quiet din of a roomful of monitors." —Children's Hospital of Philadephia website, www.chop.edu.

Learn about Penn State Children's Hospital at
www.PennStateHershey.org

In its 27th year, Global Volunteers is the pioneer in short-term, community-driven service opportunities, or "volunteer vacations". Based in St. Paul, Minnesota, Global Volunteers wages peace and promotes justice through the mutual understanding arising from shared work projects in nineteen countries worldwide. Work projects include teaching conversational English, caring for at-risk children, construction and light labor, and assisting with health care.

Learn more at **www.GlobalVolunteers.org**
or call (800) 487-1074

When Steven isn't working or volunteering, you'll find him working on projects around the house.

Johnny is advocating for kids.

Location: Houston, TX
AGE: 43
OCCUPATION: senior finance manager, Accenture

Court Appointed Special Advocates for Children (CASA)

TIME WITH THIS ORGANIZATION:
6 years

HIS TIME COMMITMENT:
2 – 30 hours per month, depending on the case

Photo: CASA

Johnny's charitable preference has always involved children. Empathetic of the fact that they don't have control over their environment, who their parents are, or the life they're born into, he was intrigued when he first learned about Court Appointed Special Advocates for Children (CASA) at a Lunch and Learn hosted at his office. After being assured by a friend that he, too, could successfully manage a CASA volunteer commitment while maintaining a busy travel schedule for his job, Johnny signed up for the training.

As a CASA, Johnny supports the work of often overburdened caseworkers. He interacts with all parties involved in the child's life, including teachers, therapists, social workers, biological and foster parents, and extended family members. Observing the child in their current home and during visitations with their biological parents, he gathers data to assess the living situation and the services most beneficial for the child and then reports his findings to the judge prior to each court hearing.

CHANGING THE WORLD ON A TUESDAY NIGHT

Johnny has advocated for children ranging in age from infant to sixteen. He's been surprised by how open and accepting the kids are, how readily they embrace him, how intense their need is to connect. The experience has opened his eyes to a hard reality, too: "You always hear or read about stories like those of these children, but you never get a full grasp of how bad the influences are out there. You really learn how abuse is truly a cycle and that the best thing to do for children is to stop the cycle for them, which will help not only them but their future children as well."

In his role, Johnny also acts as a friend and mentor. One seven-year-old boy, now living with his great grandparents, after his mother tried to commit suicide and his father tested positive for drugs, joined his first sports league. Of course, Johnny made it a point to attend all of his games.

In His Own Words:
What do you think keeps people from volunteering?
"It's the same as jumping into anything that takes time or that you know is good for you: taking the first step is the hardest part. But once you get involved, you will love it and find fulfillment in it. Live with the end in mind. When you look back on your life, what do you want to remember? It's not likely going to be your work. It will be your family and the positive impact you had on others—that will be your legacy because that positive impact will flow to their families and their children. Those are the things you're going to remember, so you want to start now to create those memories! The sacrifice of just a few hours a week versus affecting someone's whole life is well worth it."

"You can change your life by changing your attitude."
— William James

The Cause:
CASA volunteers are appointed by judges to watch over and advocate for abused and neglected children, to make sure they don't get lost in the overburdened legal and social service system or languish in an inappropriate group or foster home. The volunteers assess the best course of action and permanent placement for the children, and give their recommendations to the judge They stay with each case until it's closed and the child is placed in a safe, permanent home. For many abused children, their CASA volunteer is their one constant adult presence—the one adult who cares only for them.

Learn more at **www.NationalCasa.org**

Photo: Dan Mohr

When Johnny isn't working or volunteering, you'll find him playing sports (racquetball, tennis, golf, volleyball, mountain biking, skiing, scuba diving) or doing any adrenaline-inducing activity (his favorites to date are going on African safari and diving with sharks).

Tracy is delivering wishes & peaceful dreams

THE CHILDREN'S HOSPITAL, MAKE-A-WISH FOUNDATION

TIME WITH THESE ORGANIZATIONS:
20 years, 19 years, respectively

HIS TIME COMMITMENT:
6 – 8 hours per week

HIS ROUTINE:
Thursday nights at Children's Hospital; various home visits for Make-a-Wish Foundation

LOCATION: LONGMONT, CO
AGE: 70
FAMILY: married, father of six, grandfather of nine, great-grandfather of one
OCCUPATION: "three-quarters retired"; former technical writer and air traffic controller; now part-time flight instructor

Photo: Eric Trujillo

Every week, Tracy drives the thirty-seven miles to The Children's Hospital in Denver, to do what had previously been a paid staff position. He oversees the thirty-five other volunteers who show up every Thursday night to help sick kids feel happier and more comfortable during their hospital stay, staffing the information desk, teen lounge, gift shop, creative play center, and four playrooms.

When Tracy's Toastmasters group wanted to find a way to regularly volunteer together, their chapter president explored opportunities at The Children's Hospital. They began doing storytelling with the kids on Thursday nights, but, over the course of a year, the group thinned out, one by one, until the only person going each and every week was Tracy. "Twenty years later, Thursday nights are still my nights there. I have it on my calendar, and they count on me."

About a year into his volunteer gig at Children's, Tracy read a Reader's Digest article about the Make-a-Wish Foundation. "I had recalled seeing

CHANGING THE WORLD ON A TUESDAY NIGHT

some of their volunteers visiting with terminally ill children at the hospital, so I phoned the local office and got involved. My wife and I have delivered over eighty-five granted wishes to children in the Longmont area," he reports. In their role as Wish Granters, Tracy and his wife visit kids with life-threatening medical conditions who will be wish recipients, to help them discover their one true wish, which they communicate to the foundation. When the wish is granted, Tracy and his wife make this joy-filled announcement to the child and their family; and they, of course, are there when the limo comes to whisk the lucky recipient away for their adventure!

In this volunteer role, Tracy has to navigate the sadness that always complements the joy: "Without a doubt, the funerals of little kids is the toughest part. But we go to every one that we know of, if we've had anything to do with the family. I think it's comforting for the family. We're happy that we can be a part of wish granting. It gives the family a chance to get away for a week, and it helps to create lots of memories that may be the last wonderful memories they have to hold on to. We're proud to be a part of that."

In His Own Words:

What's the biggest thing you've learned from this volunteer opportunity?

"That we can have a whole lot more compassion for the kids; they are easier to work with than people may think. Volunteers I work with are able to handle that by putting it into perspective: you realize how lucky you are. Kids are about as tough as they can be, and they'll talk about anything with you. I've met five-year-old boys who can tell you more about what's going on with their body than the interns that work with them. It's extraordinary how much they know and accept."

"If it's worth doing, it's worth doing right."
— Unknown

What's a way that volunteering has impacted your life?

"The most amazing thing is seeing some extremely sick, bald, and frail kids just keep getting better and better. They are good fighters, and some of them eventually grow up to be healthy, productive citizens. It's been most inspiring when I see some of them return and volunteer at the hospital or through Make-a-Wish."

The Causes:

The Children's Hospital, when founded in 1908, set out to be a leader in providing the best health-care outcomes for children. That mission, still strong a century later, has consistently made them one of the top-ten children's hospitals in the nation, trusted by parents across the Rocky Mountain region. The 2008 America's Best Hospitals report, published by U.S. News & World Report, ranked them the seventh-best hospital for kids.

Learn more at **www.TheChildrensHospital.org**

The Make-a-Wish Foundation of Colorado grants the wishes of children, aged 2½ to 18, with life-threatening medical conditions to enrich the human experience with hope, strength, and joy. Since 1983, the foundation has granted more than thirty-five hundred wishes to eligible children all over Colorado. Family members and medical professionals often testify that knowing special wishes can come true has made a significant difference in the child's attitude, the family's lives, and even the child's long-term health. The wish experience gives them treasured memories and a reason to celebrate, creating hope for tomorrow, strength for today, and joy for a lifetime. The Make-a-Wish Foundation is the largest wish-granting organization in the world, with sixty-nine chapters in the United States and its territories, and twenty-seven international affiliates on five continents.

Learn more at **www.WishColorado.org** *and at* **www.Wish.org**

When Tracy isn't volunteering or working, you'll find him at the airport, flying a plane, painting landscapes, or working on a writing project.

Beverly is reading books.

LOCATION: PITTSBURGH, PA
AGE: 60
FAMILY: married, mother of two (ages 25 and 31)
OCCUPATION: psychotherapist

BEGINNING WITH BOOKS

TIME WITH THIS ORGANIZATION:
18 years

•

HER TIME COMMITMENT:
1 hour per week

•

HER ROUTINE:
Fridays 4:00 – 5:00 pm

Beverly began volunteering with Beginning with Books when her youngest child was six and she felt she had more time to give outside the home. Originally part of a literacy council, providing a literacy

CHANGING THE WORLD ON A TUESDAY NIGHT

opportunity for children of parents who were receiving literacy training, the program has expanded to serve any child whose parent feels they can benefit from a dedicated reading partner. These parents know how important reading is to their child's future success, but either don't have the time or perhaps confidence in their own reading skills.

Beverly currently reads to an inner-city boy who has grown up before her eyes: "I never really thought I'd have a close mentoring relationship with a fourteen-year-old boy or be working with the same boy for twelve years!"

Tiger's reading interests have predictably shifted over the twelve years Beverly has been reading to him. When he was little, he loved dinosaur books and went through a bug and a snake phase. In recent years, they've read the classics, and now are reading the Harry Potter series. "Tiger loves to come up and read; he really looks forward to it," Beverly remarks. "And I've recently connected him with another woman, who meets with him for vocabulary and such. She's really been helping him with his school work. He's told me that he's really glad he met me, and he thinks I'm responsible for his academic success and reading skills. He's very affectionate; it's obvious he enjoys being there at the library with me every week. It's a very special relationship."

"If you're not part of the solution, then you're part of the problem."
—Stephen Wright

In Her Own Words:

What's the biggest thing you've learned from volunteering?
"It's not anything new necessarily, but how true it is that we can make a difference in another human being's life."

What is a special moment you've experienced volunteering?
"There's an autistic kid at the library with a caregiver, and he would sometimes interrupt and want me to read his story. I explained to him politely that I was reading to Tiger. He really liked Tiger, and Tiger was always so sweet and gracious with him. While driving him home once, I commented on the way he's so respectful with this kid. He told me that he'd rather have a friend that's disabled than a friend who doesn't treat people like that respectfully."

What do you feel is the difference between donating money versus donating your time?
"Donating money is great and necessary, and we still need people to do the hands-on work. I could donate money and they can buy lots of books, but if there's no one to instill the value of reading, then the books will sit unused. It all comes down to relationship. Right now, there are more kids who want readers than we have people to read to them."

The Cause:

The mission of Beginning with Books is to meaningfully increase the number of children who become capable and enthusiastic lifelong readers. This is accomplished through research-based programs respectfully offering the information, materials, skill development, and encouragement that enable parents and other adults to promote the literacy development of the children in their care. The 'Read Together' program matches children ages 3-8 with trained volunteers who read to them, one-on-one, once a week at local libraries and after-school programs. Children form a strong bond with their adult reading mentor, gain reading experience, and learn the sheer joy of reading aloud.

Learn more at **www.BeginningWithBooks.org**

When Beverly isn't working or volunteering, you'll find her doing yoga, reading, or traveling with her husband.

Top 2 Most Common Activities of Volunteers:
1. Fundraising
2. Collection & Distribution of Food

Source: nationalservice.org

You cannot do all the good **THE WORLD NEEDS** but the world needs all the good that **YOU** can do

Sally is organizing lives.

WOMEN'S BEAN PROJECT

TIME WITH THIS ORGANIZATION:
5 years

•

HER TIME COMMITMENT:
10 hours per year

•

HER ROUTINE:
Five 2-hour weekly classes each year

LOCATION: GOLDEN, CO
AGE: 74
FAMILY: mother, 3 grown sons, 6 grandchildren
OCCUPATION: professional organizer

Sally launched her business as a professional organizer over 13 years ago. As many business owners do, she joined a professional association, the National Association of Professional Organizers (NAPO), seeking education, certification, resources and camaraderie. She found all that she sought and she got something even more, an amazing support structure and inspiration for making a difference in her own community.

NAPO has a community service program called Quantum Leap which was founded in 2000. The organization believes that people who are making big transitions in life can greatly benefit from classes that teach basic organization skills, like better management of time, paper, and personal finances. The Quantum Leap program provides free organizational skills training to people in life transitions such as; individuals living in shelters, the homeless, teenage mothers, victims of natural disasters, and many others. Professional organizers around the country volunteer their time to teach the Quantum Leap classes, some as individuals and others as part of a local chapter project.

Since the program began in 2000, over 8,000 students have been trained by professional organizers through organizations like Habitat for Humanity, Imago Dei Crisis Pregnancy Center, Dress for Success San Antonio, Katherine Hanley Homeless Shelter and in Denver Colorado Sally teaches at the Women's Bean Project.

Sally had been searching for a non-profit in her community where she could teach the Quantum Leap classes. She spoke with several organizations but hadn't found the right fit. Then she found herself on a charity event committee with Tamra Ryan, the CEO of the Women's Bean Project, whose mission is

CHANGING THE WORLD ON A TUESDAY NIGHT

"To change women's lives by providing stepping stones to self-sufficiency through social enterprise."

At Tamra's invitation Sally visited their charming facility, an old converted fire station, where dozens of women in transition are trained and employed. They work in a warehouse and office that produce a wide array of products for wholesale distribution including; salsa mixes, spice rubs, coffee beans, jelly beans, soups, chili, as well as gift baskets, baking mixes and more. This year they have just launched a new line of jewelry. Sally toured the facility and met some of the women they serve. She says she was immediately "in".

While in the program at Women's Bean Project the women learn a variety of work and interpersonal skills that they can transfer to other employment opportunities. The organization also facilitates other services that support the women during their transition, including GED and computer classes and unique offerings like Sally's Quantum Leap class.

Sally's class is offered once a year for 5 weeks. Five two-hour classes where women learn how to manage their finances, their important personal paperwork and their calendars. In Sally's class they each receive a personal calendar and a plastic crate with hanging files and file folders. When Sally asks where women are currently keeping track of their schedules and their important personal documents, she quickly learns that the skills and supplies she is providing are filling an important need. Many women share that they haven't been able to keep track of important documents, or they are simply kept in a plastic bag at a shelter or halfway house where they reside.

Supplies and materials for the classes are donated by NAPO nationally, by local NAPO chapters or by individual members. Some of the items that Sally is able to give to her class participants including; file folders, hanging folders, portable file boxes, calendars and more or donated by manufacturers like Esselte/Pendaflex and OfficeMax.

Sally enjoys knowing that her small contribution can make a big difference in the effectiveness of these women's lives. She acknowledges that this work has really opened her eyes to challenges and circumstances that people are dealing with in her community, of which she was unaware. She also admits that she finds herself very emotionally invested in the women she works with at the Women's Bean Project. She is rooting for their success, in every goal and every dream.

In Her Own Words:
What do you love about this volunteering opportunity?
"I really wanted to be able to use my professional skills and make a difference. It's really gratifying to find a place where people can really use my skills to learn how to make a better life for themselves."

What message would you give would-be volunteers?
"I would say that it may take some research, you need to explore and learn about different organizations. And find one that you are really passionate about, because when you find the cause you are really passionate about you are much more likely to stay involved with them over the long haul. It's much more rewarding."

The Cause:
Since 1989, Women's Bean Project has helped women break the cycle of poverty and unemployment. They teach job readiness and life skills for entry-level jobs through employment in their gourmet food production and handmade jewelry manufacturing businesses. Women come with the goal of transforming their lives and moving toward self sufficiency.

Learn more at **www.WomensBeanProject.com**

When Sally isn't working or volunteering, you'll find her playing outside, skiing, hiking, snowshoeing or spending time with her family.

GUITARS NOT GUNS

TIME WITH THIS ORGANIZATION:
2 years

•

HIS TIME COMMITMENT:
1 hour per week

•

HIS ROUTINE:
*Wednesdays
4:30 – 5:30 pm*

Ford is teaching guitar.

LOCATION: FALLS CHURCH, VA
AGE: 48
FAMILY: married, father of two (ages 12 and 15)
OCCUPATION: regional manager for online bookstores

Photo: Stephanie Miller

When a friend went to Africa with the Peace Corps shortly after college, Ford was intrigued by the idea of working for a common good, in a foreign environment, having to improvise every day, with little support. Eventually, family, career, and all the things that go with it made that less workable a venture, but then Ford thought, "What if I can do just a little bit in my own way?" That's what got him thinking about volunteering locally.

Ford has volunteered off and on over the last fifteen years, a few as a Court Appointed Special Advocate (CASA) for abused children, speaking for their best interests in the court system and acting as a mentor in their lives. He attained his black belt in TaeKwonDo with the goal of teaching martial arts to disadvantaged kids to help them better deal with anger issues. He's still active with Master Gardeners (about forty hours per year), teaching basic gardening techniques to adults with disabilities.

About two years ago, Ford was taken with a story in the *Washington Post* about the local sponsors of

CHANGING THE WORLD ON A TUESDAY NIGHT

Guitars Not Guns, who had channeled their very personal anger and sorrow over the accidental shooting death of a local teenager into something constructive for the community. Ford had picked up guitar a few years earlier, and though he doesn't consider himself to be "very good at it," he knew this hobby was "his little bit in [his] own way" to give back. He now teaches guitar lessons at the Boys & Girls Club in a tough neighborhood near his home. Classes last about eight weeks, and five to twelve students attend the weekly sessions.

Ford sympathizes with and admires his students: "There are stories of kids who are afraid to get up at night to go to the bathroom, because the floor in the apartment has been rented to strangers to sleep on. Some of them don't take guitars home during the program, for fear that it might be stolen on the walk home. Every child deals with their reality differently, and you will see it reflected in the classes. These kids are resilient, though."

A particularly meaningful moment was when he received a special gift from a handful of girls from a local group home. When they wanted extra study time and instruction before their final test, Ford offered to give them a couple of extra lessons at the group home, during which they made a lot of progress. A couple of weeks later, they gave him a tie-tack in the shape of the guitar. "It was a very touching gesture," Ford shares. "These are girls who I know don't have much and are facing many challenges in their lives. The fact that they put such thought and effort into something for me was very touching."

IN HIS OWN WORDS:
What message would you give to would-be volunteers?
"When it comes down to it and you've made the decision that you want to do something, do something that you really like and that you have a passion about, because it will make you more engaged and connected, on a personal level, with your cause. For me, it also helps ensure that I will find the time to volunteer."

"Wherever you go, there you are."
— Buckaroo Banzai

THE CAUSE:
Guitars Not Guns inspires at-risk and underprivileged youth to succeed by providing music education and music-career mentoring through volunteers and partnerships in their community. Providing the youth a positive alternative to the self-destructive behaviors of substance abuse, crime, truancy, and gangs, this program helps instill the confidence and character necessary to grow into responsible adults and productive members of society.

Learn more at
www.GuitarsNotGuns.org

Photo: Stephanie Miller

When Ford isn't working or volunteering, you'll find him spending time with his family, distance running, or attempting to grow tropical plants in a non-tropical climate.

Sue is baking pies.

LOCATION: DENVER, CO
AGE: 56
FAMILY: mother of three (ages 33, 35, and 36)
OCCUPATION: business owner, eco-friendly cleaning service

**SAME Café
(So All May Eat)**

TIME WITH THIS ORGANIZATION:
2 years

•

HER TIME COMMITMENT:
2 – 3 hours per week

•

HER ROUTINE:
Saturday mornings

It is easy to make a buck.
It's a lot tougher to make a difference.

Photo: Jensen Sutta

While out and about on Saturday mornings, Sue makes a phone call to Brad and Libby, the owners of SAME Café, to see if they need anything—an ingredient they're running low on, extra soup cups

CHANGING THE WORLD ON A TUESDAY NIGHT

or coffee mugs. Stopping at the local thrift store or grocery store to get it, she makes her way to the café, where patrons pay what they can afford for an organic meal, or do dishes or clean bathrooms in exchange for their food. While there, Sue tends to the café's growing plant population, occasionally adding to it, or she bakes her now-famous apple pies for the café to sell by the piece.

Sue started baking pies for the café when she decided that the menu could use another dessert offering, along with the standard sugar cookie. The owners love it and the customers love it, some getting in line to wait for the pies to come out of the oven if they know Sue's there baking. She brings all the supplies, which she purchases herself, and makes two to four pies each time—after which, she'll jump in to help with the dishes if needed.

Sue loves being part of a community. Having moved to Denver from Pennsylvania several years ago to be closer to her children, she missed the social and communal life she'd left behind. So, not only has Sue created an outlet for her love of cooking and baking, she's found a vibrant community among the staff, volunteers, and patrons of this café that has become her second home.

IN HER OWN WORDS:

What's the biggest thing you've learned from this volunteering opportunity?

"That I can do more things than I thought I could. One of the reasons I've been so involved in charity events, in addition to the café, is because it's great for networking for my own life. People who volunteer with nonprofits are, for the most part, pretty passionate about that nonprofit or they wouldn't be doing it. They're willing to spend time and spend money as well. They're not just donating their time, but donating their resources and being willing to use their influence with other people in the community. My former employer donated $3000 this past year, at my recommendation. They have a grants program, so they give every year, but they had never given to this organization until I nominated them."

What do you think keeps people from volunteering?

"I think it's the same reason people don't give: they haven't been asked. They don't know what volunteering opportunities are out there. They don't know their skills are needed and can make a difference. They don't think they have anything to give, so they don't get involved. They don't go looking, but they wouldn't turn it down if someone approached them."

What message would you give to would-be volunteers?

"You can use your gifts and talents to help other people. Think of things you really enjoy doing, or are good at doing, and find an organization that needs those things. Sometimes their needs are publicized and sometimes they aren't. Call and ask if you can be of service there."

THE CAUSE:

SAME Café aims to build a healthy community via their philosophy that everyone—anyone who walks through their door—regardless of economic status, deserves to have their basic need for food met in a respectful and dignified manner. Unique in its lack of a set menu and set prices, SAME Café prepares its food based on the daily availability of fresh, organic ingredients. Instead of a cash register, a donation box is available for patrons to pay what they feel their meal was worth or a little more to help cover for those less able to pay. Diners who can't pay are encouraged to exchange an hour of service.

Learn more at **www.SoAllMayEat.org**

When Sue isn't working or volunteering, you'll find her hanging out with her family, walking at the park, perusing the bookstore, catching a baseball game, or planting flowers on her patio.

Katrina is teaching chess.

LOCATION: Portland, OR
AGE: 44
FAMILY: married, mother of two (ages 11 and 13)
OCCUPATION: full-time mom

Katrina had happily witnessed the changes in her sons' maturity and confidence over the two years they'd been participating in the Chess for Success program at their elementary school. So when the coach position, a paid role generally held by a teacher, remained vacant in the fall of 2003, Katrina stepped in to run the program on a volunteer basis.

CHESS FOR SUCCESS

TIME WITH THIS ORGANIZATION:
5 years

HER TIME COMMITMENT:
5 hours per week

HER ROUTINE:
Mondays & Wednesdays, after school, October through March

Photo: Stephen Funk

CHANGING THE WORLD ON A TUESDAY NIGHT

Though she was still recovering from treatment for breast cancer—surgery, six rounds of chemotherapy, six weeks of radiation—she didn't miss a day that year. Since then, she's made it one of her highest priorities and even took on the position at a second school during the two years her older son attended middle school.

For the last five years, Katrina has coached up to one hundred students per year. Some have competed at the state level; some had never played chess before joining the club. She really enjoys seeing how they improve over the year—as players, learning how to move the pieces to implementing complex strategies, and as human beings: "I know that it really helps improve self-esteem. Children who play chess also tend to perform better on math tests. I've seen children who you'd never guess could learn to play chess because they have trouble reading and writing or lack social skills."

Katrina knows the kids are learning some great metaphors for life: managing a problem one step at a time, exercising patience to win, planning ahead, and slowing down to think about what you're doing before taking action.

She also knows that all good things have a ripple effect. One year, a fifth-grade boy, new to the school, joined Chess for Success, and his little brother, a kindergartener, technically too young for the program, would tag along. After a few weeks of losing every game he played, the older boy started winning, and his play improved so much over the year that he qualified for the regional tournament. Similarly, his younger brother initially didn't say a word, though he was always cooperative and followed directions; by the end of the year, he was talking and actually had won a couple of chess games. Katrina later found out that they had moved from a Native American reservation, about 100 miles away, to Portland so that their mom could participate in a residential alcohol rehabilitation program. Neither of the boys had ever played chess before participating in Chess for Success, and the older boy had improved his game by teaching residents in the rehabilitation community how to play chess!

"You can't play good chess fast."
—Jack Weeks

In Her Own Words:
What message would you give would-be volunteers?
"If you volunteer for something, it doesn't mean it's a lifetime commitment."

The Cause:
Chess for Success (CFS) is not a chess club; it's an educational program that uses chess to teach children high-level thinking and social skills—skills necessary for success in school and life. CFS currently serves thirty-two hundred elementary and middle school students in eighty-three schools in sixteen school districts in Oregon and Washington. All students receive fifty hours of after-school chess instruction, T-shirts designed by club members, and chess sets to take home at the end of the year. Schools receive chess sets and demonstration boards for their club, and a chess library for the school.

Learn more at **www.ChessforSuccess.org**

When Katrina isn't keeping up with her boys or volunteering, you'll find her sewing purses, watching romance movies, camping in the tent trailer with her family, or competing on a dragon boat team with fellow breast cancer survivors.

―――――― is
――――――
――――――.

LOCATION:
AGE:
FAMILY:
OCCUPATION:

Your picture here

ORGANIZATION:
――――――

TIME WITH THIS ORGANIZATION:
――――――

•

TIME COMMITMENT:
―― *hours per* ――

•

YOUR ROUTINE:

YOUR STORY:

CHANGING THE WORLD ON A TUESDAY NIGHT

IN YOUR OWN WORDS:
What message would you give would-be volunteers?

Favorite quote:

THE CAUSE:

When _____ isn't volunteering, you'll find her/him _____

Resources:

For Volunteers—Places to find opportunities:
Volunteer Match: www.VolunteerMatch.org
All for Good: www.AllforGood.org
Hands On Network: www.HandsonNetwork.org
Idealist: www.Idealist.org
United Way: www.UnitedWay.org
The Corporation for National and Community Service: www.serve.gov
UN Online Volunteering: www.OnlineVolunteering.org

Skills-Based Volunteering:
CatchaFire: www.CatchaFire.org
Taproot Foundation: www.TaprootFoundation.org

No-commitment Volunteering:
One Brick: www.OneBrick.org

Resources for Families:
www.DoingGoodTogether.org
www.VolunteerFamily.org

Volunteer Vacations:
Global Volunteers: www.GlobalVolunteers.org
International Volunteer HQ: www.VolunteerHQ.org
uVolunteer: www.uVolunteer.org

Micro-Volunteering:

The Extraordinaries—It's a website and a mobile phone application. Allowing people to use their spare time for unique micro-volunteering projects done completely online or from your phone. www.BeExtra.org

It Starts With Us—Join the A-Team, as they work together to change the world! You'll get one email per week with an assignment that takes just 15 minutes or less to complete. With all of us working on it together, we accomplish some very big things. www.itstartswith.us

Ordinary People Change the World—One Dollar. One Deed. One Day. Find lots of small ways you can make a difference. www.OrdinaryPeopleChangeTheWorld.com

Jumping In With Both Feet:

Give a year or two—has this book inspired you to give more than one night a week? Perhaps you're considering giving a whole year or two to be of service.
If so, we recommend exploring possibilities with the PeaceCorps, AmeriCorps, CityYear and Mercy Volunteers.
www.PeaceCorps.gov
www.AmeriCorps.gov
www.CityYear.org
www.MercyVolunteers.org

Non-profit Jobs:

Inspired to make a career change to the non-profit sector? Find non-profit job listings at:
www.Idealist.org
www.NonprofitJobs.org
www.JobsinNonprofits.com
jobs.change.org
www.OpportunityKnocks.org

OnaTuesdayNight.com

Visit the official site for videos,

more resources, more stories,

cool gear, and a place to

share your own experiences!

Find Your Cause

Gandhi said "Be the change you wish to see in this world."

What is the change you would like to see?
A great place to start is to review the profiles in this book that moved and inspired you the most and visit the websites of the non-profits. Read about the organizations, look at their pictures, watch their videos, read their mission statements.

I wish...

If you had one wish for the world, what would it be?
_____

The world just needs more... _____

What I value most is... _____

What values are most important to you? _____

❏ Love ❏ Justice ❏ Compassion ❏ Security ❏ Family ❏ Happiness
❏ Respect ❏ Freedom ❏ Health ❏ Peace ❏ _____

I love...

What I appreciate most about my life is _____

What aspects of your life bring you the most joy and/or fulfillment?
❏ Arts/Crafts ❏ Animals ❏ Nutrition/Cooking ❏ Music
❏ Outdoors ❏ Friends ❏ Children ❏ Health & Fitness
❏ Sports ❏ Books ❏ Family ❏ _____

How could you share these things that you love the most or have more of them in your life?
_____
_____

Where do you have the most fun?
Indoors or Outdoors _____ With people, things or animals _____

This worksheet is designed to help you discover what stirs your heart, what you are most passionate about, to help you find your cause.

I feel...

FOLLOW YOUR HEART AND YOUR PASSIONS:

As you go about your life and interact with others, read stories and watch news reports....

What moves you? _____

What grabs your attention? _____

What fires you up? _____

What makes you angry? _____

What makes you sad? _____

I can...

YOUR SKILLS AND TALENTS:

The skills and talents that I have that I currently am not using are...

_____

_____

The skills and talents that I use regularly and really enjoy are...

_____

_____

What would you do for a living even if you wouldn't get paid for it?

_____

_____

The kinds of organizations that I would imagine could use these skills & talents are...

_____

_____

I AM DRAWN TO THESE TYPES OF CAUSES:

❏ Animals ❏ Arts & Culture ❏ Children & Youth ❏ Criminal Justice ❏ Disaster Aid
❏ Economic Development ❏ Education ❏ Environment ❏ Health & Disease
❏ Homeless/Housing ❏ Human Services ❏ International ❏ Mental Health
❏ Religion ❏ Seniors ❏ Sports & Recreation ❏ Veterans ❏ _____

GETTING CONNECTED...

A great next step would be to visit www.VolunteerMatch.org or one of the other sites listed on the Resources page—enter your zip code and enter in some of the keywords that showed up in your answers to these Find Your Cause questions. Review all of the search results and see what inspires you!

GETTING STARTED...

If you're still not sure of the type of causes you would like to serve, we recommend getting involved with a service organization that donates time with lots of different charities and organizations. Once you are in action, you will find the types of volunteer work that inspire you the most. Check with your local non-profit association or volunteer organization. See the Resources page for websites that can direct you to these groups.

I Will...
_____
_____
_____
_____
_____
_____
_____
_____
_____
_____

........come alive.

"Do not ask yourself what the world needs; ask yourself what makes you come alive. And then go and do that. Because what the world needs is people who have come alive."

— Harold Whitman

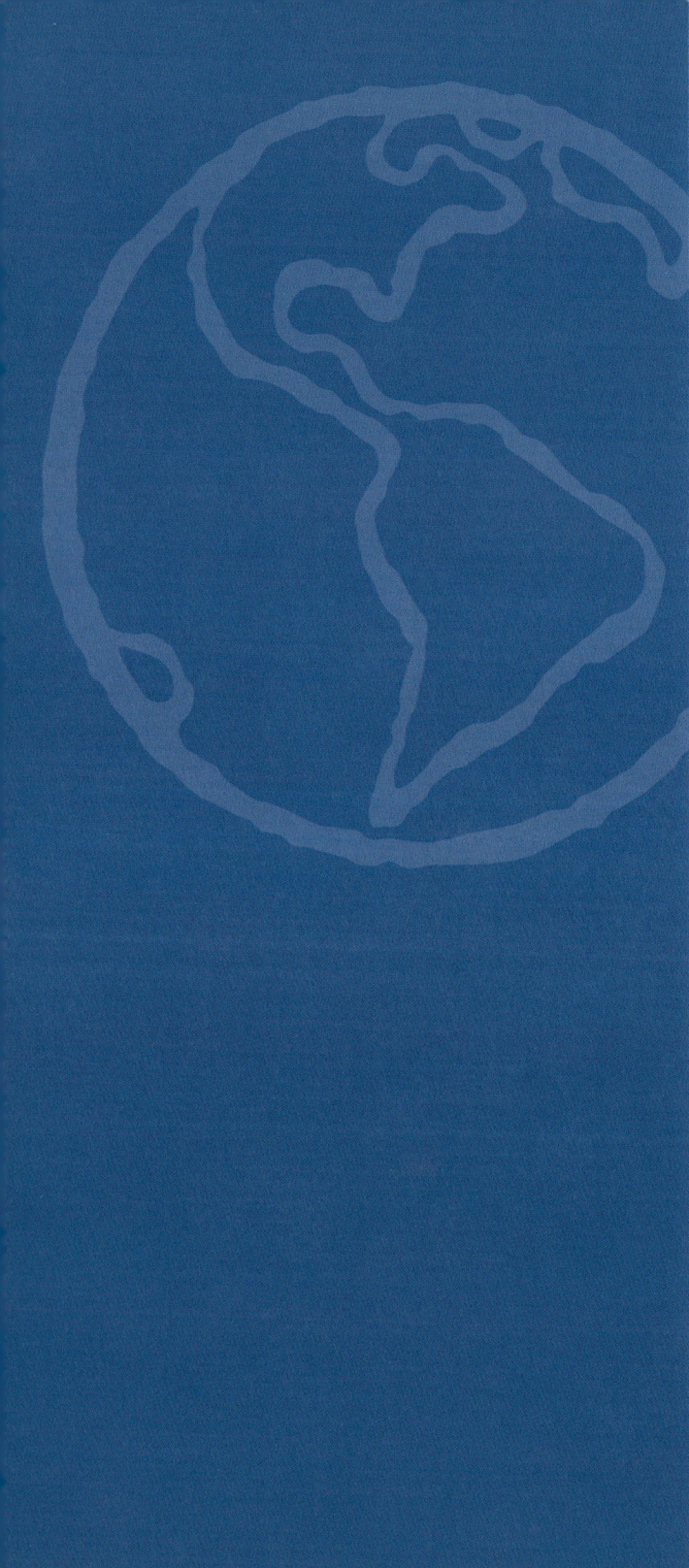

Acknowledgements:

They say it takes a village to raise a child, and I can say it certainly takes a large tribe to birth a book. Some contributions were made over a period of years, some months, some weeks and others just a moment of contribution that made a world of difference. I am equally grateful to each and every one of you. Thank you for your love, commitment, creativity, and generosity. My intention is that this book makes a huge difference in the world and that intention would not have the opportunity to be fulfilled without your contributions.

This book would not look or sound anywhere near what it looks and sounds like without; my creative, committed, impeccable editor Marj Hahne, my passion-filled, visionary graphic designers Eric Trujillo and Mandy Oscarson, and my uber-creative, inspiring illustrator Kelly Rodrigues. I am forever grateful for your partnership, your commitment, and your faith in this project and in me.

To Jason Greager, thank you for the huge amount of faith you've had in this project, for being one of my biggest and most enthusiastic cheerleaders and for inspiring me to dream the biggest possible dreams.

To Alecia Huck, Gerry O'Brion, Reece Salinas and Chad Steele, there is not room on this page to detail all of the ways that each of you made a difference for me, and truly there aren't even enough words in the world to express what your love and support means. Thank you for believing in me and keeping me focused on my commitment.

This book would never have been possible, in it's current form, without the following people. Thank you, from the bottom of my love-filled heart, to Torrey Lippincott, Jonny Dalrymple, Larry Byram, Mike Valentine, Fabio Cardosa, Tracy Castelli, Ron DeVille III, Bridget Burton, & Laura Murray.

Thank you to all of the volunteer coordinators and executive directors at the wonderful non-profits featured in this book. Thank you for the time and attention you gave to help connect me with the perfect volunteers to interview.

Thank you to the inspiring group of talented and generous photographers from around the country who gave of their time to capture the beautiful faces of the volunteers I interviewed.

And of course, thank you to the volunteers I had the privilege of interviewing. Thank you for sharing your stories, thank you for inspiring others and thank you for the difference that you make in the world.

PHOTOGRAPHY:

Thank you to the generous, talented photographers who captured all of the beautiful faces of the volunteers I interviewed. If you are in need of a photographer, please consider doing business with these amazing big-hearted people!

Location	Photographer	Website
Madison, AL	Nicole Allen	www.NicoleAllenPhotography.com
Phoenix, AZ	Pamela Nicole Bernasconi	www.PamelaNicole.com
Los Angeles, CA	Leontine Wallace	www.LeontineWallace.com
San Diego, CA	Robert Weeks	www.RobertWeeksPhotography.com
San Francisco, CA	Erica Carillo	
Denver, CO	Eric Trujillo	www.StudioTrujillo.com
Denver, CO	Jensen Sutta	www.JensenSutta.com
Stamford, CT	Lindsay Comer	www.LindsayComer.com
Washington, DC	Stephanie Miller	www.SMillerPhotography.net
Honolulu, HI	John De Mello	www.JohnDeMello.com
Iowa City, IA	Dawn Frary	deweystreetphotocompany.wordpress.com
Chicago, IL	Brandon Williams	www.blackgreeksonline.net
Kansas City, KS	Megan Barnes	www.StudioEmebee.com
Louisville, KY	Sarah Hester	www.SSHPhotography.com
Boston, MA	Bill Burke	BillBurke.photography.com
Annapolis, MD	Stephanie Miller	www.SMillerPhotography.net
Savage, MN	Dan Buettner	www.PicsByDan.com
Raleigh, NC	Dan Glasgow	www.danglasgow.com
Omaha, NE	Tree DeAngelis	www.CapturedByTree.com
Danville, NH	Jane Lydick Staid	www.JaneLydickStaid.com
Santa Fe, NM	Spencer Wright	
Las Vegas, NV	James Tanksley	www.JamesTanksleyPhotography.com
New York City, NY	Anthony Saint James	www.AnthonySaintJames.com
Cincinnati, OH	Nicole Jones	www.NJonesPhotos.com
Portland, OR	Stephen Funk	www.StephenFunkPhotography.com
Philadelphia, PA	Missy Sowden	www.SSPhoto.com
Pittsburgh, PA	Richard Schultz	
Providence, RI	Brad Smith	www.SmithBrad.com
Houston, TX	Dan Mohr	www.DanMohrPhotography.com

About the Author

Tammi DeVille is changing the world every Monday morning, when she spends thirty minutes mentoring a thirteen-year-old boy in South Africa, via webcam, through an organization called Infinite Family. She also donates time to Art from Ashes, an organization that empowers struggling youth through creative programs. She has been volunteering on a consistent basis, while working full-time, for the last eight years.

Tammi's other volunteering activities have included facilitating a writers' group for homeless women at a local shelter, advocating for two-and-a-half-year-old twins through CASA as a court-appointed special advocate, and mentoring two teenage girls through Colorado Youth at Risk. All these opportunities have required no more than two hours of her time each week. She anticipates many more volunteering adventures in her future.

Tammi is an ordinary person, perhaps like you, busy making a living—currently as an author and a small business consultant—while dreaming of ways to make an even bigger difference in her community and the world. She currently resides in Denver, Colorado.

Buy *Tuesday Night* Gear!

Did you enjoy Kelly Rodrigues' inspiring QuoteArt throughout the book? You can own all kinds of cool gear adorned with that art! Wear your heart and your commitment to service on your sleeve…or your coffee mug, mousepad, messenger bag…. Visit **www.OnATuesdayNight.com** to learn more!